THE ESCAPE OF
CHARLES II

THE ESCAPE OF CHARLES II
AFTER THE BATTLE OF WORCESTER

STRATFORD-ON-AVON

LONG MARSTON

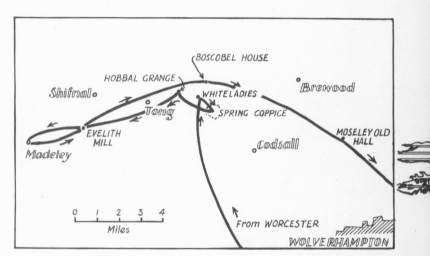

HOBBAL GRANGE

BOSCOBEL HOUSE

Shifnal

WHITELADIES

Brewood

Tong

SPRING COPPICE

EVELITH MILL

MOSELEY OLD HALL

Madeley

Codsall

0 1 2 3 4
Miles

From WORCESTER

WOLVERHAMPTON

Neale House
AMESBURY

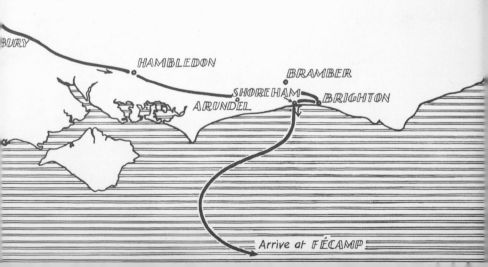

BURY

HAMBLEDON

BRAMBER

SHOREHAM

BRIGHTON

ARUNDEL

Arrive at FÉCAMP

THE ESCAPE OF CHARLES II

After the Battle of Worcester

by

Richard Ollard

CHARLES SCRIBNER'S SONS
New York

TO
MARY

PREFACE

THE STORY of Charles II's adventures after the Battle of Worcester on Wednesday, September 3rd, 1651, is treated in almost every work on that far from neglected monarch. What excuse can there be for a book devoted exclusively to this subject? In the end the only answer to this question is the book itself: like every other, it must stand or fall on its own merits. I can however give some account of my reasons for writing it. First, and first by a very long way, is that the story is such a fascinating one; and second that it has never had justice done to it. Most recent works dealing with the subject seem to me cavalier both in their sympathies and in their treatment of evidence; in any case the whole episode is usually, and, given the terms of reference, rightly, handled as a curtain-raiser to a reign that was deficient neither in incident nor romantic interest. Of the two works which explicitly confine themselves to the King's escape, Mr. H. P. Kingston's admirable *The Wanderings of Charles II in Staffordshire and Shropshire after Worcester Fight* (Birmingham, 1933) only concerns itself with the opening phase of the story. And Allan Fea's *The Flight of the King* (London, 1897) is more in the nature of an extended commentary on the invaluable collection of sources there reprinted, and reflects its author's predilections for topographical and genealogical detail. Much of the topography has inevitably been overtaken by the passage of time. What was a saddler's shop in 1897 is probably a launderette today and may be a car-park tomorrow. I have made no such attempt; and it would have been irrelevant to my purpose to trace the living descendants of the people about whom I have written.

To tell the story I must interpret evidence and portray character. I have tried to do both with fidelity and the minimum of fuss. The note on sources at the end of the book will nearly always make it plain, if the context does not, from what source I have drawn my material. Where there is any possibility of doubt I have cited my authority. If I have had to guess at anything I say so, and in one or two places I have briefly interrupted the narrative to criticise the evidence.

In the matter of dates I have followed the established convention of using the English month date (which, in the seventeenth century, was ten days behind the calendar in general use abroad). In the spelling of names, if in nothing else, I can claim to have caught something of the atmosphere of my period which disdained a slavish consistency. The general principle I have aimed at has been to use the form most familiar to modern readers. Similarly in quotation I have generally, but not always, modernised spelling and punctuation. For those who require a brief statement of the background to the story I subjoin a historical note.

I should like to express my thanks to my brother Christopher and to Professor Michael Lewis for reading my manuscript and making a number of valuable suggestions; to Sir Owen Morshead for his company in tracing the King's journey through Dorset; to Mr. Michael Robinson of the National Maritime Museum and to Mr. David Piper, Director of the National Portrait Gallery, for enlightening my ignorance on several points. Their kindness, I need hardly say, renders them in no way responsible for the shortcomings of this book.

CONTENTS

ILLUSTRATIONS

KEY TO ACKNOWLEDGMENTS

[1] Lord Sackville: photograph by George P. King, Sevenoaks
[2] By gracious permission of Her Majesty the Queen
[3] National Portrait Gallery
[4] Mr. Nicholas Hudleston: photograph by the Royal Academy of Arts
[5] Ashmolean Museum: photograph by the Courtauld Institute of Art
[6] British Museum
[7] Plymouth City Art Gallery: photograph by Tom Molland Ltd., Plymouth,
by permission of Miss J. M. Dean
[8] Ministry of Public Buildings and Works: Crown copyright reserved

HISTORICAL NOTE

CHARLES I had been executed in January 1649, the Monarchy and the House of Lords had been abolished, and England had been proclaimed a Commonwealth. During the closing stages of the Civil War when defeat had become certain Charles I had sent his two eldest sons out of the country, so that Charles II succeeded to the throne while in exile in France. The divisions of the victorious party led the Scotch Presbyterians, who had not been consulted in the trial and execution of Charles I, to invite Charles II to return to his northern kingdom, on terms which involved a betrayal both of the principles and of the people hitherto identified with the Royalist cause in Scotland. Against the advice of Clarendon and all his most trustworthy servants Charles accepted and landed at Speymouth in June 1650. Politically the venture turned out as Clarendon had said it would: militarily it resulted in Cromwell's defeat of the Scots at Dunbar in September 1650 and the subjugation of the greater part of Scotland. Charles's only hope now lay in leading whatever Scottish army he could muster into England and rallying support amongst the Cavaliers and others who disliked the Commonwealth Government. He crossed the border in July 1651 and reached Worcester at the end of August. Again Clarendon, who had always set his face against any attempt to win the struggle in England by employing outside forces, was proved right. Bringing the Scots into England in the seventeenth century was like bringing the Russians into Central Europe in the twentieth. The inhabitants regarded them as backward and barbarous. In consequence the Royalist army received little accession of strength as it made its way down the western side of England. Cromwell's victory at Worcester strengthened his already formidable political position. In 1653 he became Lord Protector – that is, virtually Dictator – and remained in unassailable power till his death in September 1658. After eighteen months of confused political manoeuvring Charles II was restored in May 1660.

I

Introductory

WHATEVER VIEW one takes of Charles II it seems clear that his experiences in the six weeks that followed the Battle of Worcester were crucial to the formation of his character and to the development of his political principles. To be a hunted man concentrated the mind just as wonderfully as the knowledge that one is to be hanged in a fortnight. That he himself regarded it as the central episode of a not uneventful career can hardly be doubted. It was the principal topic of his conversation aboard the *Naseby* (by then renamed the *Charles*) as she carried him back to England in May 1660. Twenty years later he dictated a long and vivid account to Pepys. And in the intervening period he had shewn in a hundred ways, from his scheme for a new order of chivalry that would commemorate the oak in which he took refuge at Boscobel to his keen interest in the paintings and writings which dealt with his adventures, that the subject was never far from his thoughts. Like the rest of his dynasty he was not, as a rule, conspicuous for remembering past services, but the men and women who had assisted his escape did not find themselves forgotten.

At first sight it seems natural that so fascinating and exciting a story should exert its compulsion over its principal character. But is this really so? People who have worked in resistance movements or prisoners-of-war who escaped do not generally care to dwell on their experiences. What is thrilling to the reader was frightening to the man he is reading about. Fear

[15]

of detection, of exposure, of humiliation, of prison and of public execution, these must have been the King's unsleeping companions. The people who helped him did so at the certain risk of death for themselves and ruin for their wives and children: that can hardly have been a pleasant thought. And permeating the whole affair was the vile smell of defeat: a beaten army, a forsaken cause, a King who would count himself lucky to escape to the barely civil hospitality of France and the futile squabbles of his mother and his ministers. Why should any man, let alone one who professed and acted on the belief that pleasure was the chief end of life, choose to remind himself of such sombre passages in it?

The most convincing explanation is that these six weeks saw him at his best and that he himself recognised this. Although he was only twenty-one this was to be the high-water mark of his qualities, not touched again. He was to display again, notably in the face of the virulent political agitation to exclude his brother James from the succession to the throne, the same courage and coolness; but these virtues were then disfigured by a cold acquiescence in judicial murder and a cynical indifference to the sufferings of innocent people. He was to display again – Halifax, one of the ablest of his ministers and most penetrating of observers, thought too often again – his remarkable power of concealing his thoughts and emotions. He retained to the end of his life the affability and ease of manner, the total absence of shyness, that perhaps no English monarch has possessed in the same degree. His most universally endearing characteristic – the ability to stand outside himself and offer polite, amused comments on what he saw – was as evident in his deathbed apology for being such an unconscionable time a-dying as in his comment on his portrait as a young man: "Odds fish, what an ugly fellow I am", or in his supremely graceful farewell to the Stafford-shire peasants who, having guided him at night through a particularly dangerous and difficult stretch of country, had

[16]

quietly turned for home to be recalled with the words "My troubles make me forget myself: I thank you all". All that was likable or admirable or striking in the King's character showed, in this testing time, to best advantage: all that was base lay dormant or accepted the discipline of his situation.

Beside the fact that his ordinary qualities here appeared at their brightest, one cannot read far in the story of Charles's adventures without recognising that he possessed unusual talents for clandestine activities. How unusual becomes evident if we compare the conditions of the seventeenth century with our own time. The success of the spy, the underground activist or the man on the run depends, obviously enough, on not drawing attention to himself, which in turn depends on not showing self-consciousness or unfamiliarity in going through the routine motions of the ordinary everyday things of life. Nowadays a President or a Prime Minister who found himself under the unfortunate necessity of making for the nearest frontier would probably experience no difficulty in changing a wheel or using a public call-box. The social system of the seventeenth century rendered it unthinkable that a man born to great place should have acquired such a familiarity. At about the same time as the events described in this book France was the scene of the confused and factious civil wars known collectively as the Fronde. In the course of these the great general Condé suffered defeat and had to escape in disguise. According to his friend and ally Mademoiselle de Montpensier he chose the character of a groom and was very nearly detected when, being sent to the stable to saddle and bridle a horse, he proved incapable of doing either. Charles, as we shall see, nearly gave himself away on at least one occasion by his ignorance of everyday things: but his coolness and resource saved him from suspicion.

The great secret of his success was that he was a natural actor of uncommon quality. Sharpness of observation, mimicry, a sense of timing, an awareness of the effect he was producing on his audience, all these gifts can be instanced from other passages in his life. But only here can be seen that zest in projecting oneself into another's character, that exhilaration in being rid of one's own too familiar personality, without which acting is nothing. In all his roles, from the eloping lover to the Puritan drawling disapproval of drunken oaths, Charles obviously enjoyed himself. In all of them his uninhibited performance made the task of his helpers a hundred times easier.

Enough has been said to justify the claim that the King's talents and virtues were seen at their brightest in his hour of extreme danger. And memory must have intensified their lustre in contrasting the period that lay behind and before. Charles's experiences in Scotland had been deeply unhappy. To get there in the first place he had been forced into the betrayal of Montrose, the bravest and most brilliant of his champions. This proved to be only a down-payment in dishonour; the Presbyterians extorted incessant instalments; the King found himself not only impotent and disregarded, he was forced to listen, even on occasion to assent, to the most humiliating, indeed insulting, attacks on his father and his mother. And even then he had to watch while his tedious mentors threw the game away. Exactly a year before the Battle of Worcester Cromwell had been outmanoeuvred at Dunbar by David Leslie, a professional soldier of solid if unexciting quality. Total defeat was, humanly speaking, inevitable. But fortunately for Cromwell human speech was not the only medium available. The fatuous conceit of the divines led them to overrule the carnal wisdom of their general with catastrophic results. The detestation of Scotland that Charles retained to the end of his life can hardly be wondered at.

The eight and a half years of exile that followed his escape were less odious but more demoralising. At least in Scotland there had been an army, even if he did not command it: there had been resources, even if he did not control them: there was always tomorrow. Back on the Continent there was only the morning after.

II

Worcester

ARLY ON the morning of September 3rd the King
climbed the tower of Worcester Cathedral to view the
situation and to hold a council of war. It was a fine day
and the elevation of the vantage point, the sudden withdrawal
into the fresh, still air from the clatter and confusion of men
preparing for battle may have induced a feeling of mastery
over events. If it did, the sight that met his eyes can have
done little to confirm it. To the south and east Cromwell's
main army was drawn up on the rising ground that covered
the road to London: to the south-west Fleetwood was putting
in a sharp attack across the Teme, the north bank of which was
held by the Scots infantry under Montgomery. This force was
now being threatened in the rear by a strong detachment under
Cromwell's personal command who were throwing a bridge
of boats across the Severn only a mile or so below the city.
The only Royalist troops in a position to dispute the passage
were the small band of three hundred Highlanders under
General Pitscottie. Except in courage the two sides were not
evenly matched. Cromwell was soon over the Severn and more
and more of his troops poured across after him. About the
same time or shortly after, Fleetwood forced the passage
of the Teme, driving Montgomery, who was running short of
ammunition, back into the city.

It was at this point that the Royalist commanders delivered
a counter-stroke that deserved better fortune. Recognising
that the transfer of so many men to the west bank of the

[20]

Severn must have weakened the main force to the south and east, they abandoned the security of the city walls and marched out of Sudbury Gate to launch a frontal attack. This spirited move was at first successful. The Parliamentary troops wavered and then gave ground. The Royalists captured some artillery, an arm in which they were totally deficient except for sixteen leather guns, a form of light field-piece that bore the same relation to the real thing as a tent does to a house. In this attack Charles distinguished himself by his fearlessness and dash, "having led out the army, and engaged it himself, charging at the head thereof many several times in person, with great courage and success", to quote the letter of an unknown Royalist who was captured after the battle and imprisoned at Chester. The same writer concludes his account of the battle with the following tribute, the more telling for the circumstances in which it was written:

"And of his royal person I can give no farther account; but certainly a braver prince never lived, having in the day of the fight hazarded his person much more than any officer of his army, riding from regiment to regiment, and leading them upon service with all the encouragement (calling every officer by his name) which the example and exhortation of a magnanimous general could afford; showing so much steadiness of mind and undaunted courage in such continual danger, that had not God covered his head, and wonderfully preserved his sacred person, he must in all human reason needs have perished that day."

Had these attacks been supported by the Scottish cavalry who had so far taken no part in the battle it is possible –most of the English Royalists would have said certain – that the King would have carried the day. They made no attempt to do so. David Leslie, their commander, was no Marshal Ney. As a professional soldier he can hardly have felt much confidence in the haphazard conduct of the campaign; as a shrewd and somewhat detached observer he would not have missed

[21]

the significance of the King's failure to attract any accession of strength during the long march through counties generally credited with Royalist sympathies; as the veteran of many battles he might not unreasonably conclude that this one was lost and that the problem of extricating his force and getting it back through two hundred miles of hostile country would become impossible if once he committed it to a general action. He was much abused for his caution at the time: and when, after the Restoration, he was created Lord Newark, the King was told that he should rather have hanged him for his old work.

Cromwell, on the other hand, had been quick to see what was happening. Recrossing the Severn and recalling several of the regiments which had followed the retreating Scots, he soon gained the upper hand, drove the Royalists back "at push of pike", to quote his own description of the close fighting, and battered the city with his artillery. It was about five o'clock in the afternoon and the battle was won. Charles arrived back at the Sudbury Gate to find it blocked by an overturned ammunition wagon. He had to get off his horse and climb over the shafts and the dead oxen that had been pulling it. As soon as he was in the city he took off his armour: it was a hot day and the weight must have been irksome. Many of the soldiers who had got back into the town before him were throwing down their arms. Finding a fresh horse, the King rode up and down among them, his hat in his hand, urging them to stand and fight. "I had rather you would shoot me, than keep me alive to see the sad consequences of this fatal day." But it was no good. Cromwell's troops had stormed the fortifications and were pouring into the town, as were Fleetwood's from the other side. Although it was to be several hours before the last stronghold was reduced it was already high time to be gone if the victory were not to be crowned by the capture of the King.

The only route left open was that to the north. Charles

accordingly slipped out by the St. Martin's Gate, whether on foot or on horseback is not clear. According to some accounts he had returned briefly to his lodging and escaped by the back door as Colonel Cobbett, one of the Parliamentary commanders, entered by the front. If this is true, and the total lack of preparation for the King's personal safety makes it perfectly credible, then he can hardly have found his horse conveniently waiting for him over the garden wall. What is certain from his own account and many others is that as soon as he was clear of the city he was joined by his servants and all the principal noblemen and gentlemen who had survived the battle. Prominent among them were Derby, Lauderdale, Buckingham and Wilmot, later Earl of Rochester, who was to be his constant companion in the adventures that lay ahead. "I found them", Charles told Pepys, "mightily distracted, and their opinions different, of the possibility of getting to Scotland, but not one agreeing with mine, for going to London saving my Lord Wilmot; and the truth is, I did not impart my design of going to London to any but my Lord Wilmot. But we had such a number of beaten men with us, of the horse, that I strove, as soon as ever it was dark, to get from them; and though I could not get them to stand by me against the enemy, I could not get rid of them, now I had a mind to it."

Even in the first few minutes of his new career as a wanted man Charles had shown an impressive grasp of the most important principles: to get rid of companions who were not strictly necessary and to keep one's mouth shut about one's own intentions. His choice of London as an objective also showed much better judgement than the preponderant preference for Scotland. Not a single one of the fugitives from Worcester succeeded in getting there, though most of them made for it. London, on the other hand, was much the safest place for a man who was trying to escape the attention of the authorities. So huge a place offered, before the days of an

[23]

organised police force, an ideal sanctuary. And its pre-eminence as a port made secret communication with the Continent comparatively easy.

The dilemma of the King's immediate destination was resolved by Lord Derby. Having decided to head north, the King and his party of notables branched off to the right of the main road along which the mass of the Scottish cavalry were plunging. A trooper of Lord Talbot's regiment who was said to know the country well was appointed guide, but soon after darkness had fallen the poor man confessed himself totally lost. They were in fact a few miles short of Kidderminster, where Richard Baxter, the Presbyterian divine, was then living. His *Diary* gives a brief, vivid glimpse of what was happening that night. He had just gone to bed when he heard the noise of a large body of cavalry in disorderly retreat. A small detachment of one of Cromwell's regiments stationed themselves outside Baxter's house, called on the fugitives to halt and fired on them. There were only thirty Cromwellians, but the beaten cavalry, who numbered several hundred, could not tell in the dark how many there were. They panicked and surrendered in large numbers. Charles's instinct to keep clear of a demoralised army was sound.

In the agitated discussion taking place a few miles to the south, Lord Derby suggested that the King should make for Boscobel, a house that lay deep in Brewood Forest, some fifteen miles from where they then were. Lord Derby had recent experience of its merits as a hide-out. On his way to join the King's army at the head of a small party of Royalists he had had the misfortune to run into a Commonwealth regiment just outside Wigan. His force was defeated and scattered and he himself was badly wounded. Making his way painfully to the south he arrived at Boscobel, where he was so well looked after that in a few days he was strong enough to join the King at Worcester. The house had two great recommendations besides its remoteness and the fact that it

[24]

was surrounded by the woods that had given it its name:[1] being well to the west of the road to Scotland it suggested the much more attractive possibility of an escape into Wales, where Royalist sympathies were strong and Commonwealth troops few and far between; and, best of all, its owners, the Giffards, were a staunchly Roman Catholic family whose long experience of concealing priests and evading the recusancy laws made them, in the circumstances, ideal hosts.

Charles leapt at the idea. Second only to the disadvantages of his own princely upbringing was the fact that his friends were all much too respectable. In Church and State they represented the established order, or had done until the day before yesterday, and their habits of life and cast of mind were not to be changed in a hurry. Forging papers, wearing disguise, hiding people, diverting suspicion under interrogation, all these necessary arts of the conspirator were scarcely conceivable to them. With the Roman Catholics, or recusants as they were generally called from their refusal to attend the public worship of the Church of England, this was not so. Nearly a century of persecution had given them a wealth of such experience. Had the King not had the luck to find himself in the hands of such seasoned campaigners at the very outset of his adventures it is probable that his enemies would have caught him.

By a further stroke of luck it turned out that Mr. Giffard was himself among the sixty or so Cavaliers who were riding with them. He was presented to the King and suggested that his servant, Francis Yates, should act as guide. Yates, alone of all the men and women who helped the King to escape, was subsequently executed for refusing to give information. A route was quickly agreed on which would take them through Stourbridge and then to the edge of the forest where Yates's local knowledge could lead them along tracks and by-roads.

[1] *Bosco bello:* the beautiful wood. The name had been suggested by a guest at the original house-warming party.

Stourbridge was the first town they had had to pass through. To avoid detection or suspicion it was determined that they should only speak French as they clattered through the streets, an eloquent comment on the notions of security to be expected from the King's adherents. No one challenged them. Soon after, they left the road for the comparative safety of the woods.

About three o'clock in the morning they arrived at White-ladies, another house belonging to the Giffards, which was only about half a mile from Boscobel. Giffard may well have thought it an even better place, as being smaller and less comfortable and therefore less likely to attract immediate attention. It was to prove an excellent decision.

The noise of the hooves on the drive and the insistent knocking on the door brought a man to an upstairs window. Had they any news of Worcester fight? They had indeed. The front door was quickly opened and Charles, Derby, Giffard and a few others admitted. As soon as Giffard had told the man who Charles was, the door was opened again and the King's horse, blown after more than forty miles of hard riding, was led into the hall. The man whose reflexes were as quick as that was no amateur. He was, in fact, George Penderel, the first of five brothers all living on the Giffard estate who were to contribute more than any other family to the King's preservation. Like their landlord they were recusants and strong Royalists – a sixth brother had been killed fighting for Charles I. Two of the brothers were sent for at once – William, who lived at Boscobel itself, and Richard, who lived at a small farm called Hobbal Grange. Meanwhile everything had to be done urgently. George Penderel knew that there was a detachment of Commonwealth troops at Codsall, only three miles away, and the disturbance caused by this large body of horsemen might bring them along at any minute. The first thing to do was to get rid of every single one of the King's companions. This was made slightly easier by the arrival of the news that David Leslie with three thousand of the Scottish horse were close to Tong Castle, only two miles to the west. It was even suggested to the King that he should join them and attempt to force his way to Scotland: but Charles having rejected this course immediately after the battle did not see any reason to change his mind. It did, however, provide an obvious rallying point for his supporters, and in a short time most of them, led by the Earl of Derby, rode off to find Leslie's troops, taking the King's horse with them. The few, the very few, who decided to get away on their own were the only ones who in the end avoided capture.

Before leaving, Lord Derby called William and Richard Penderel into an inner room where the King was and urged them to take as good care of him as they had of himself only a few days earlier. By this time dawn was already breaking and a hiding-place had to be found without delay. As he came into the house Charles had snatched off his George[1] and entrusted it to Colonel Blague,[2] emptied his pockets of gold, which he distributed amongst his servants, and had given his watch to Lord Wilmot. He also started to take off his clothes, and Richard Penderel, as soon as he arrived, was sent back to Hobbal Grange to bring a spare suit of working clothes. Somebody cut off most of his hair and he was told to rub his hands against the back of the chimney and then to apply them to his face. A coarse shirt was provided from the resources of the house. Shoes were a difficulty. The only ones available were a vile fit. To a man escaping on foot this was a serious handicap. And Charles had already resolved to walk to London, a decision he communicated only to Lord Wilmot who, it was agreed,

---

[1] The badge of the Order of the Garter worn on a ribbon round his neck.

[2] This jewel rejoined its owner on the Continent after a journey almost as eventful as his own. Blague buried it under a heap of rubble near the house in Staffordshire where he was caught and sent to the Tower of London. It was shortly afterwards brought up to him by Izaak Walton. Blague then escaped from the Tower and restored it to the King in person.

should remain in the neighbourhood till the King was safely on his way and should then meet him in London at the sign of the Three Cranes in the Vintry.

Dressed as a woodman and equipped with a billhook, Charles was hurried out of the back door of Whiteladies into a wood called Spring Coppice. Richard Penderel accompanied him and tried to make him as comfortable as possible. Hardly had they got into the wood before a steady downpour set in, so Richard went back to the house to fetch a blanket for him to sit on. Charles's chief memory of the day, apart from the rain, was of extreme hunger. All his life he enjoyed an appetite remarkable even for that age when calories and carbohydrates lay beyond the horizon of dietetic curiosity. On this occasion it must have been uncommonly sharp. There could not have been much opportunity of eating during the battle on the previous day. We know that there was none on the long night ride, except for a crust of bread and a can of beer outside an inn near Stourbridge. And all he was given when he got to Whiteladies was a glass of sack and a biscuit. Probably the last meal he had had was breakfast on the morning before. Thirty years later he could still remember how ravenous he was. ''In this wood I staid all day, without meat or drink,'' he told Pepys. His recollection does not quite do justice to Richard Penderel. Without saying anything to the King he sent his sister, Mrs. Yates, into the wood with a dish of scrambled eggs. The King's pleasure at this seasonable relief was tempered with alarm that a woman of whom he knew nothing should know where he was hiding. ''Good woman,'' he said to her, ''can you be faithful to a distressed Cavalier?'' ''Yes, sir,'' she answered, ''I will die rather than discover you.''

When she had gone Charles was left to the sound of the steady dripping from the leaves and to the company of his thoughts. What these were we know from his own account. When he was making his way into the wood with Richard Penderel early in the morning he had questioned him anxiously

[28]

about what men of quality he knew who lived on the way towards London. He didn't know any. This was a blow. In spite of the ideal nature of the country for a man on the run it was clearly imperative to get away from it as soon as possible. The place was alive with troops. They were no sooner in the wood before Charles saw a party of cavalry go past along the road. If London was ruled out, and the road to Scotland was already choked with Leslie's men and their pursuers, that left Wales. The more he thought about it the more sensible it seemed. The principality was only lightly held; there were plenty of Royalists there; Swansea was a port through which there was a considerable trade with France. By the time Richard Penderel came to fetch him in the evening he had made up his mind to try and cross the Severn that night.

III

Friends in Need

W HILE THE King was dividing his mind between dry
clothes, roast joints, and the possibilities of escaping
into Wales, his friends the Penderels were anxiously
occupied. William, Humphrey and George acted as scouts and
look-out men, while Richard was immediately responsible for
the King's safety. John Penderel had, however, the most
dangerous assignment, that of looking after Lord Wilmot.

Wilmot, who was the companion of Charles's adventures
from first to last, provided the strongest argument for the
theory, early advanced and long maintained by pious Royalists,
that the King's preservation can only be explained on the
hypothesis of direct Divine intervention. Except for personal
courage and invincible self-confidence he had none of the
qualities or aptitudes required in their situation. And he had
a number of terrifying defects. He was stupid, he was careless,
he was forgetful, he was indiscreet. He was determined on no
account to forgo the style of life to which he was accustomed
as an officer and a gentleman, blandly refusing to move from
place to place except on horseback. He also declined absolutely to entertain the idea of any disguise, although on a
subsequent secret mission to England in 1655 he won some
reputation for his versatility in this respect, appearing sometimes in the character of a Frenchman with a yellow periwig
and sometimes as a grazier with a basket-hilted sword tied up
his back. Even on that occasion he was luckier than he deserved. He was actually caught at Aylesbury and only managed

to escape to London by bribing the man to whose custody he had been confided: once in London he attracted the attention of the authorities again and would certainly have been arrested if Colonel Hutchinson, that paragon of Republican virtue, had not tipped him off, a piece of work that came in handy at the Restoration when Hutchinson was in danger of execution as a regicide. Clarendon, who did not like Wilmot, sourly observed of these exploits that "in making his journeys . . . he departed very unwillingly from all places where there was good eating and drinking". In an earlier passage of the *History of the Great Rebellion* Clarendon has painted a double portrait of Wilmot and Goring which is one of the acknowledged masterpieces of that incomparable gallery. A dissolute *bon vivant*, he was evidently a popular messmate in the Royalist armies. No doubt he had been so too in the Dutch cavalry regiment where he had learned his trade of soldiering.

He was the type of man that Charles throughout his life found most congenial: easy, licentious and convivial. At twenty-one the comradeship of a man of the world nearly twice that age who flatters one into a sense of equality is irresistible. Above all he personified Emancipation. No one could have been less like a Scots Presbyter. No one could have been less like the grave and sedate noblemen to whom Charles I had entrusted the upbringing of his son. No one was more openly disapproved of by Clarendon and the old sobersides who were always counselling caution and delay, who had advised strongly against the venture that had ended so disastrously at Worcester the day before, and who were on this and every other occasion so maddeningly right. These considerations would have qualified Wilmot, had he survived the Restoration, to shine at the court of which his son[1] was to be so distinguished a member. They were not, however, much to

[1] If, indeed, he was his son. See C. V. Wedgwood, *The King's War* (London, 1958), p. 663, note 149.

the present purpose. The King's choice of Wilmot as his companion and chief agent, even more his persistence in that choice after that nobleman had shown himself something of a liability, was the only mistake he made in the whole affair.

Meanwhile on that Thursday morning it was John Penderel's task to convey an aggressively conspicuous Royalist mounted on an expensive but tired horse to a place of safety through a countryside bristling with enemy troops. Matters were not made any easier by Wilmot having no clear idea of where he wanted to go. They set off in a northerly direction and were in trouble almost at once. As they passed Brewood Forge the smith and his mates, who could tell from a glance at the horses all they needed to know, came clattering out in pursuit. Fortunately a friend of the Penderels who happened to come by at that moment assured them that the Royalist officer with his servant was in fact a Cromwellian colonel and they gave up the chase. A few minutes later they narrowly escaped meeting a party of troops on the march. John Penderel had had enough. He turned off the road and led Wilmot into a disused pit belonging to a neighbouring farmer. Wilmot would have to get off and walk. The horses were taken to a second neighbour's barn and a lodging for Wilmot was found at the house of a third.

Thankful to be relieved, for a time at least, of so splendid an encumbrance, John Penderel hurried off to Wolverhampton to see if he could find safer quarters for him. On the contrary, the town was full of soldiers. Stopping at a farm on his way back to make discreet inquiries of a friend, he had his first piece of luck. A tall, good-looking man was coming down the road with a parcel under his arm. They recognised each other at once and stopped to talk. John Penderel asked if there were any news. Excellent news, the other replied, the King had won the day at Worcester. John quickly disabused him and went on to tell him of Charles's arrival at Whiteladies – was it only that morning? – and of his present whereabouts. More important to his immediate concerns, he went on to tell him about Wilmot and to ask his advice and help. It was not surprising that John should show such a total lack of reserve, for the man he was talking to was a Roman Catholic priest, educated and ordained at Douai and later to become a member of the Benedictine order. Both for his personal experience and for his probable contacts he was exactly the man for the present crisis.

Who was he and what was he doing in that part of the country? His name was John Huddleston and he was the younger son of a landed family in Lancashire. He had been born and bred a recusant: his elder brother had accompanied him to Douai and his uncle had been one of the Benedictines of the English mission. During the Civil War he had fought in the King's army. He was at this moment living at Moseley Hall, a few miles to the south-east of Boscobel, the house of his co-religionist Mr. Thomas Whitgreave, where he was discharging the dual functions of domestic chaplain and tutor to three young Catholic gentlemen, two of whom were Whitgreave's nephews. It was indeed to collect six new shirts for himself and his pupils that he had gone out that afternoon.

No sooner had Huddleston heard John's story than he offered to take him to see his host, Mr. Whitgreave, who would very likely be able to help. They set off at once for Moseley, where Whitgreave without a moment's hesitation suggested that he should accompany them to Wilmot's lodging and arrange for him to take up his quarters at Moseley. John Penderel's relief at this turn in affairs can have been equalled only by the alacrity with which Wilmot accepted the prospect of exchanging a modest yeoman's house for the comforts of Moseley Hall. These comforts included, as he was to discover on his arrival there that night, a "privacie" or hiding-hole for priests in which the owner had successfully concealed himself when the house was violently searched by Parliamentary troops at the end of the Civil War. He was so delighted with it that he expressed the wish that a hundred thousand of his friends were with him, so difficult did he find it to distinguish between the convivial and conspiratorial aspects of life. The phrase must have startled Whitgreave: he remembered it when he came to write his account some thirty years later. He had already had some experience of Wilmot's talent for making a mess of things. At their meeting that afternoon Whitgreave had carefully worked out a route along by-paths for Wilmot and his present host to take and had made a rendezvous for midnight in a field near the house. After waiting there fruitlessly till two o'clock in the morning he had concluded that Wilmot must have changed his plans. Returning to his house he found him comfortably installed. His guide had taken him direct along the public highway and he had not seen anything wrong or thought it necessary to have Whitgreave brought back from the rendezvous.

On one point, fortunately, Whitgreave had been adamant. Moseley Hall stood too close to the public road to allow him to extend its hospitality to Wilmot's horses. He therefore sent over to a neighbour, Colonel Lane of Bentley Hall, to ask if he could stable them. Colonel Lane replied that he would be delighted to do so and that as he had commanded a regiment in Wilmot's brigade during the war he would like to come over the following evening to see his old comrade-in-arms and discuss a very promising scheme for furthering him on his journey. Wilmot did after all have one priceless advantage – luck.

If John Penderel's day spent in settling Wilmot's affairs had been a long one, so had the King's. About five o'clock Richard Penderel came to fetch him to his house, Hobbal Grange, where they could have a meal before starting out on their night journey towards Wales. As they walked, Richard had to keep correcting the King's gait, which was markedly not that of a labourer. The accent presented comparatively few difficulties. Charles was a natural actor and mimic and, as an early narrative puts it, "his most gracious converse with his people in his journey to and at Worcester, had rendered it very easy and very tuneable to him". The meal at Hobbal Grange that night was not very substantial – a fricassee of bacon and eggs. Charles however did not let his hunger prevent him from being a most agreeable guest. He talked to Richard's little daughter and took her on his knee: and he made himself pleasant to old Mrs. Penderel, the mother of the five brothers, who came to see him and to give him her blessing.

As dusk fell Richard and the King set out. They had decided to make for the house of another recusant, Francis Woolf, at Madeley, a place about nine miles to the west, from which it would be easy to cross the Severn. They found the going rough and heavy, plunging through swampy ground, wading streams, forcing a way through thorn hedges. The King's shoes rubbed his feet raw. For the only time on the whole expedition he gave way to despair, throwing himself on the ground and saying that he would rather stay there till daybreak and be caught than go a step further. Richard showed tact and resource "sometimes promising that the way should be better, and sometimes assuring him that he had but little farther to go". Two miles short of Madeley they had to cross a small river by means of a mill-bridge. Richard opened the gate across it, but instead of shutting it softly let it snap back. At once the miller appeared in the doorway, his white clothes gleaming in the dark, and challenged them. Not being satisfied with Richard's answer that they were neighbours going home, he called for help to some people inside the mill whom both Richard and the King took to be soldiers. They ran for it up the lane, a lane which Charles remembered as "very deep and very dirty". At last, out of breath, they lay down behind a hedge and stayed quiet for half an hour until they were quite sure that there was no pursuit.

An hour or two later they arrived at Mr. Woolf's house.

[35]

Charles hid behind a hedge while Richard went to the door. Mr. Woolf, roused from sleep, was far from enthusiastic. Two militia companies were quartered in Madeley: the bridges over the Severn were all closely guarded, as were the ferries for several miles up and downstream: to harbour a Royalist fugitive was much too dangerous: Mr. Woolf would not venture his neck for any man, unless it were the King himself. Richard replied that was exactly who it was, and the startled Mr. Woolf began to make hurried preparations for receiving him. Charles, when told of this exchange, was very put out, as he had given Richard no authority to reveal his identity. Yet it is very difficult to see what else he could have done; dawn was not far off, Woolf was obviously anxious to get back to bed and bolt the door, there were troops all round and the King was, by his own account, in no condition to go much further. Anyway there was no alternative now and Charles went into the house and was given some cold meat which must have been very acceptable. The house was provided with several priests' holes, but all had been discovered in the constant searches to which Mr. Woolf had been subjected. It was therefore considered safer to put the King in the barn behind the corn and the hay. The day passed uneventfully, except for several conferences with Woolf which confirmed a unanimous opinion that Wales must be abandoned and that they should therefore return to Boscobel that night. The King's mind reverted to his original plan of making his way to London.

With the fall of darkness they slipped out of the barn and into the house. A meal had been prepared against their journey; and Mrs. Woolf, who had noticed that the colour of the King's hands did not match that of his face, prepared an infusion of walnut leaves. Should they walk or ride? Woolf and Richard Penderel both thought it safer on foot. It says a good deal for Charles's self-command as well as for his understanding of his situation that he should have accepted this decision without protest when his feet, rubbed raw from yesterday and still imprisoned in those unspeakable shoes, must have been agony. One can't see Wilmot accepting such uncongenial advice from a peasant and an old codger.

Richard and the King set off about an hour before midnight. Charles was determined at least to avoid sprinting about in total darkness pursued by irate millers. He suggested to Richard (who could not swim) that they should ford the river, and went in first. Luckily it was only waist-deep, but it can hardly have added to the comfort of the journey. About three o'clock on the Saturday morning they were close to Boscobel and Richard, leaving the King in the wood, went ahead to get intelligence. In the house he found a redoubtable friend to the King's cause, Colonel William Carlis,[1] who had fought at Worcester so tenaciously that he had stayed to see the last man killed. Escape, left so late, had been correspondingly difficult and Carlis, a member of a Staffordshire recusant family, had thought that William Penderel would be able to hide him at Boscobel till the hue and cry was past. A hue and cry there certainly was: both the house and the woods surrounding it were likely to be searched during the day that was just coming on.

For the moment, however, the coast was clear. The two Penderels, together with Colonel Carlis, went back into the wood to fetch Charles. Breakfast consisted of bread and cheese. As a special luxury William Penderel's wife made the King a posset of thin milk and small beer – a dispiriting beverage, one would have thought, on which to face the rigours of the day. More to the point, she warmed some water to bathe his feet while Carlis pulled off his shoes and stockings. Both were sopping wet and the shoes were full of gravel. As there was not another pair in the house that would fit him – not that

[1] Or Carless. The family subsequently changed its name to Carlos, at the King's suggestion, to commemorate the close tie between the Colonel and himself.

these did – Mrs. Penderel put some hot cinders in them to dry them and, after washing his feet, provided him with a clean pair of stockings. It was now high time to be taking cover. Colonel Carlis had already selected a tall oak, standing by itself with a good all-round view, whose lower branches had been lopped and whose top bushed out so thickly as to render anyone in it invisible from below. Carlis and the King climbed into it by means of William Penderel's wood-ladder. Provisions – the inevitable bread and cheese and small beer – were passed up to them, together with a couple of pillows, as Charles had now been three nights without sleep, and the ladder was withdrawn. Sure enough the military were soon upon the scene. "While we were in this tree," Charles told Pepys, "we see soldiers going up and down, in the thicket of the wood, searching for persons escaped, we seeing them now and then peeping out of the wood." This did not prevent him from falling into a profound slumber, his head on Carlis's arm which after a time became numb. This put the Colonel into a quandary. If he were to speak to the King loud enough to wake him he risked discovery. So he very sensibly woke him by pinching him. A generation later Dr. Plot in his *Natural History of Staffordshire* pointed out that though the oak that sheltered the King was in the county of Salop "yet even there he rested in the lap of a *Staffordshire* Gent".

Meanwhile the Penderel family went about the King's business with their usual enterprise and coolness. William and his wife kept peeking up and down in the wood to see what the soldiers were up to. Richard was sent to Wolverhampton to buy wine, biscuit and other small luxuries not generally to be found on the tables of Boscobel or Whiteladies. Humphrey, the miller, was dispatched to the local militia headquarters ostensibly to pay the levy due for maintaining a soldier, but in fact to find out all he could about the plans and intelligence of the enemy. While he was handing over the money to the captain on duty, to whom he was known, in came a Cromwellian colonel who, in the manner of senior officers down the ages, began barking out a series of brisk and disconcerting questions. Was not this house Whiteladies known to be a nest of Papists and persons disaffected to the Government? What measures had been taken to search it? What measures were proposed to search it? Had the captain personally investigated? For once the captain was one up on his superior. If the colonel wanted information about White-ladies he had come to the right address. The man waiting for his receipt was the miller there, one of a family of brothers employed by Mr. Giffard, the owner.

The colonel rounded on Humphrey. Did he realise that the penalty for harbouring those who had taken arms against the state was death? He did. Had he heard that a reward of a thousand pounds had been offered for the apprehension of the King? He had not. A cannonade of questions followed which Humphrey countered by pleading ignorance but, skilfully, not too much ignorance. A crowd of Cavaliers had, he admitted, turned up at Whiteladies on the morning after the battle and he had heard that the King was among them. But wherever he was he certainly was not there now. How could he be? There were three separate families living on top of each other in the house, all of them perpetually squabbling. Concealment in such a household was simply impossible. The colonel was impressed by the sense and apparent candour of Humphrey's replies. He bustled off to pursue his inquiries elsewhere while Humphrey returned to Boscobel.

Over supper that evening, a meal for which a couple of chickens were provided, he described his interrogation. At the mention of the price put on his head Charles was observed to look dismayed. To people as poor as the Penderels a thousand pounds was unimaginable wealth. Humphrey noticed the King's change of expression and was embarrassed. Colonel Carlis took the bull by the horns and told the King in front of them all that "if it were one hundred thousand pounds, it

[39]

were to no more purpose, and that he would engage his soul for their truth''. Charles was reassured and the Penderels saw that he was. This was the only occasion on which he allowed, for a moment, his face to betray him.

He and the Colonel had come down out of the oak as soon as it began to get dark. Considering the unremitting nervous strain and the sheer physical exhaustion of the past three days he was in very good spirits, joking while Carlis superintended a further assault on his hair by William Penderel armed with a pair of shears. (In spite of strict instructions to burn what he had cut off William treasured it – occasionally, in later years, parting with a lock or two to those who would pay such a relic the veneration due to it.) Charles's principal anxiety was to re-establish contact with Wilmot. Not, as he explained to Pepys, that he wanted to join forces with him, but to keep him informed of his reversion to his original plan of making for London and to restore their rendezvous at the Three Cranes in the Vintry. His wish, however, could not be satisfied that night. John Penderel, who had originally been assigned the responsibility of looking after Wilmot, had been summoned to attend him at Moseley Hall the day before and had not yet returned. Probably he would be back in the morning: and if he was not, William or Richard could easily slip over to find out what Wilmot was up to.

Before retiring for the night Charles was asked what he would like for his Sunday dinner and expressed a preference for mutton. This caused the Penderels some embarrassment, as butcher's meat was far beyond their means. William and his wife had not tasted mutton since the merry-making at the christening of their eldest child. If they were suddenly to go out and buy some now it would be certain to attract notice. Colonel Carlis solved their problem for them by creeping out before dawn to a neighbour's sheepcote and sticking his dagger into the best lamb he could find. He and William carried it home and flayed it and the King himself cut the meat into what he called Scotch collops and fried them to the admiration of the company. The farmer, on being offered compensation for the theft a day or two later, refused when he heard that the meat had been required for a fugitive from Worcester.

Meanwhile the King passed a most uncomfortable night in a hiding-place between two walls which was not long enough for him to lie down in. Still it was secure enough: and if ease of body was impossible it must have been some consolation to know that the Penderel family, reinforced by Colonel Carlis, were there to keep trouble at bay.

IV

A Warm Scent

WHILE THE King had been undergoing all these discomforts and dangers Lord Wilmot had found out a
more excellent way. Or to be more exact, he had
had one found for him. His old companion-in-arms, Colonel
Lane of Bentley Hall, who was stabling his horses for him, had
produced a heaven-sent chance of escape. His younger sister
Jane had a particular friend, Mrs. Norton of Abbots Leigh near
Bristol, who was expecting a baby and had asked if Jane could
come and stay with her over the birth. This had all been
arranged, and a pass for Jane and a manservant to accompany
her obtained from the local Parliamentary commander, before
the Battle of Worcester had been fought. It thus provided a
foolproof means of getting a man right out of the danger zone
and leaving him in a safe house – for the Nortons, like the
Lanes, were strong Royalists – within easy reach of the second
busiest port in the country. Wilmot, recognising how precious
an opportunity offered, felt that the King ought to have first
refusal of it. He sent John Penderel over to Whiteladies for
news that same night (Friday) and he was not expected back
until the small hours of Saturday morning. He therefore
thanked Colonel Lane for his offer, told him that he was well
satisfied with his present quarters, and asked him to keep the
opportunity open until he heard from him again. A few hours
after Colonel Lane had started back to Bentley, John Penderel
returned to Moseley with the news that Charles had left for
Wales on Thursday night. Now that the King was out of

[42]

reach there was no point in not closing with Colonel Lane. Wilmot asked Whitgreave to send a servant over to Bentley to tell Colonel Lane to bring his horses over that very night – Saturday – but kept John Penderel in ignorance of his plans and his destination. He kept him in attendance on him throughout Saturday, finally releasing him from his responsibilities late that evening.

The hour or two that it took to walk from Moseley to Boscobel must have been for John Penderel a period of deliciously relaxing tension. He was done with Wilmot – at any rate nothing had been said about his coming back; and the King was now two days journey away in Wales. There might be some nasty moments ahead if and when the Government picked up the trail and started asking questions. But they would cross that bridge when they came to it. Really there was nothing to stop life at Whiteladies and Boscobel resuming its normal tranquillity. It must have been a shock to hear on arrival that the King was back again and had spent the day hiding in an oak tree.

The first immediate consequence of this was that John Penderel had to return to Moseley early on Sunday morning. The King was impatient to co-ordinate his plans with Wilmot's; and Wilmot should in any case be informed without delay of his master's situation. As he came close to Moseley Hall he saw Whitgreave and Father Huddleston walking in the garden, and hurried up to them to ask where Wilmot was. They answered that he had gone but, veterans of the Roman Catholic underground, did not say where. Penderel's reply shook them: "We then are all undone." And he went on to tell them that the King was back at Boscobel after his unsuccessful attempt to cross the Severn. Such grave news suspended the rules of underground security. Without a moment's delay[1] Whitgreave

1 Thus Whitgreave in his own narrative. But in the *Summary of Occurrences* which he wrote jointly with Huddleston ". . . having first offered to God their Sunday Duty for his majesty's safety". Huddleston in his own *Brief*

and Huddleston took John Penderel off to Bentley Hall (they had to go themselves because he and Colonel Lane did not know each other and the situation was much too critical to risk any misunderstanding). There they found Wilmot, who had arranged to leave for Bristol with Jane Lane the next morning. This was at once postponed and Wilmot agreed with Whitgreave that the danger of leaving the King in so deeply compromised a house as Boscobel was so great that he must be moved to Moseley that very night. Wilmot would ride over to join him there, accompanied by Colonel Lane who could take the horses back to Bentley. John Penderel could work out with Whitgreave and Huddleston the details of the King's route and method of transport. Even at this crisis Wilmot was not prepared to walk.

John lost no time in getting back to Boscobel. After the discomforts of the night and the excitements of the past week the King was passing a tranquil day. It was observed that he spent a long time over his prayers, after which he took a book into a secluded corner of the garden. No search parties disturbed the peace of that long autumn Sunday, whose stillness was heightened by the distant sound of the bells of Tong church. The only alarm was caused by the King's falling into a sudden fit of nose-bleeding. Carlis and the Penderels were apprehensive; illness of any kind would make their task ten times more difficult. But Charles reassured them by telling them that he often had these attacks and had never suffered any ill-effects.

John's return raised everybody's spirits. Not only was there

Account is even more emphatic on the point. "Then Mr. Huddlestone took him [John Penderel] to his Chamber and bid him rest there till we had performed our Dutys to God for his Majesty's Preservation and Safety, it being Sunday, bid him rest himself well, his obedience in that would be more acceptable to God than his Prayers though Sunday, for he had laboured all that night and the day before; Rest was more necessary and we would pray for him."

now a plan, instead of an increasingly threatening question-mark, but, even better, it was to be put into almost instant execution. John had agreed to a rendezvous with Whitgreave, but the details of the journey had still to be arranged. Who was to go with the King? Were his feet sufficiently recovered for a five-mile walk, and if not, where were they to find him a horse? Charles, believing that the smallest escort was the safest, asked that he might be accompanied only by John and Colonel Carlis. The Penderels were not at all in favour of this idea, first because Carlis was well known in the district as a wanted man, and second because the troops were so thick on the ground that they might well run into a patrol, in which case numbers would be an advantage. Charles accepted this and it was agreed that he should be escorted by all the five Penderel brothers together with their brother-in-law Francis Yates. He resisted, however, their evident preference for walking: the agony of the journey to Madeley and back was still too vivid and his feet were still raw. They relented as to the first half of the journey but insisted that the final approach to Moseley must be made on foot. That still left the question of how to get hold of a horse and a saddle and bridle in the few hours before they were due to start. Eventually someone suggested the cart-horse Humphrey Penderel used for carrying sacks from his mill. An extremely decrepit saddle and bridle were found and the animal was brought round to the gate about eleven o'clock.

Charles took an affectionate farewell of Colonel Carlis who, after a few weeks, was to succeed in escaping to the Continent. He then mounted and set off through the woods, two of his escort marching ahead, two behind and one on either side. Each of them was armed with a long billhook or a pitchfork, the nearest they could get to a pike, and some had pistols in their pockets. The general effect must have resembled the party of Masetto's friends in the second act of *Don Giovanni*. The early illustrations of the scene which appeared soon after

[45]

the Restoration all have an irresistible air of *opéra bouffe*. Yet it was the only occasion throughout the King's journeyings on which he relied on force rather than deception as his first line of defence. A party of peasants, armed to the teeth, moving stealthily along woodland paths in the middle of the night, simply could not hope to pass themselves off as law-abiding citizens going about their ordinary business. Luckily they did not meet anyone.

After they had covered a mile or so Charles complained jokingly that his mount "was the heaviest dull jade he ever rode on". To which Humphrey the miller, who owned him, replied with a prompt wit that must have pleased the King: "My liege, can you blame the horse to go heavily when he has the weight of three kingdoms on his back?" This repartee was treasured by the family, who were careful to remind the King of it when they came to visit him at Whitehall after his Restoration. They soon reached Pendeford Mill, which was the point from which the Penderels wanted the King to complete his journey on foot. John and Richard and Francis Yates were to see him safe to the rendezvous with Whitgreave, while William, Humphrey and George led the horse back to Boscobel. Charles dismounted and, anxious to get the last lap over, set off briskly with his guides. Suddenly he was conscious that three men who, poor as they were, had risked their all for him without any thought of reward, had turned for home without his saying a word of thanks or farewell. Their exquisite manners challenged his own. He turned back and caught them up. "My troubles make me forget myself," he said, "I thank you all," and gave them his hand to kiss.

Wilmot had by this time arrived safely at Moseley and had sent Colonel Lane back to Bentley with the horses. As the minutes passed he grew more and more agitated and kept fussing Whitgreave and Huddleston to go and see if "his friend" as he called him were in sight. Whitgreave took up his station in the orchard and presently saw them coming up the long walk. When Charles came up to the door, Whitgreave tells us, he was so effectively disguised that "I could not tell which was he, only I knew all the rest". This is not only a striking tribute to the thoroughness and intelligence of the Penderels but of particular interest as the earliest first-hand evidence, though recorded a good many years later, of what Charles looked like when he was on the run. It certainly confirms that he had the true actor's ability to look the part. Father Huddleston, who met him a few minutes later, supplied Pepys with a detailed description which is perhaps worth giving at length.

"The habit that the King came into Father Hodlestone was a very greasy old gray steeple-crowned hat, with the brims turned up, without lining or hatband, the sweat appearing two inches deep through it, round the band place; a green cloth jump coat,[1] threadbare, even to the threads being worn white, and breeches of the same, with long knees down to the garter; with an old sweaty leathern doublet, a pair of white flannel stockings next to his legs, which the King said were his boot stockings, their tops being cut off to prevent their being discovered, and upon them a pair of old green yarn stockings, all worn and darned at the knees, with their feet cut off; which last he said he had of Mr. Woolfe,[2] who persuaded him thereto, to hide his other white ones, for fear of being observed; his shoes were old, all slashed for the ease of his feet, and full of gravel, with little rolls of paper between his toes, which he said he was advised to, to keep them from galling; he had an old coarse shirt, patched both at the neck and the hands, of that very coarse sort which, in that country, go by the name of hogging-shirts; which shirt, Father Hodlestone shifting from the King, by giving him one of his new ones, Father Hodlestone sent afterwards to Mr. Sherwood,

[1] A kind of short coat common in the seventeenth and eighteenth centuries.

[2] The King's host at Madeley.

now Lord Abbot of Lambspring, in Germany . . . who begged this shirt of Father Hodlestone; his handkerchief was a very old one, torn and very coarse, and being daubed with the King's blood from his nose, Father Hodlestone gave it to a kinswoman of his, Mrs. Brathwayte, who kept it with great veneration as a remedy for the King's evil;[1] he had no gloves, but a long thorn-stick, not very strong, but crooked three or four several ways, in his hand; his hair cut short up to his ears, and hands coloured; his majesty refusing to have any gloves, when Father Hodlestone offered him some, as also to change his stick.''

This disreputable figure was at once taken upstairs where Wilmot was awaiting him while Whitgreave took the Penderels into the buttery for something to eat and drink before they went home. The servants were all in bed and, it was hoped, asleep, so it was Father Huddleston who was sent down to summon Whitgreave to the presence of his guests. Wilmot could not resist dramatising his own fitful observance of the requirements of security. "This gentleman under disguise," he announced, "whom I have hitherto concealed, is both your master, mine, and the master of us all." This can hardly have been news to Whitgreave; indeed Wilmot himself had explicitly instructed John Penderel to tell Whitgreave after their interview at Bentley earlier in the day, if indeed it is conceivable that he had not already done so when he arrived distraught with anxiety to find Whitgreave and Huddleston strolling in the garden at Moseley. Whitgreave knelt down and kissed the King's hand. Charles, after suitably gracious remarks and promises, at once asked "Where is the private place my lord tells me of?" On being shown it he went in and expressed the greatest satisfaction. It was a very different affair from the Little Ease of Boscobel. Although dark

[1] Scrofula, a disease for which the Sovereign's touch was long considered the best remedy. Queen Anne was the last monarch to touch for the evil and Dr. Johnson was one of her less successful patients.

Charles II about 1650

From a painting after the portrait by Hanneman.

A view of Boscobel, Whiteladies and the Royal Oak by Robert Streater.
Almost certainly commissioned by Charles II about 1670.

On the left the ruins of the Cistercian convent (still standing), on to which is
built the half-timbered house of which no trace now remains. In front a troop

of horse, the King's fellow fugitives, ride away in improbably good order. There are two figures in the garden of Whiteladies representing the King and Richard Penderel on their way to hide in Spring Coppice. Separated by woods (now cut down), to the right of the picture stands Boscobel House—in reality about a mile away.

Richard Penderel

Father Huddleston

Jacob Huysmans

Wilmot as a young man

Jane Lane

Bentley Hall.

*From the engraving
in Plot's Natural
History of
Staffordshire.*

and airless it was, by the standards of such places, spacious; and the approach to it, by means of a secret door in the panelling into a bedroom and from there through a trapdoor in the floor of a cupboard, gave the hunted animal the reassurance that its burrow was secure. It was a boon granted in the nick of time, for the next two days were to bring the hunt close to its quarry.

No wonder that Charles, as he came back into the parlour, felt expansive and that his spirits rose visibly. While Father Huddleston bathed his feet, which were still very sore and inflamed, Whitgreave provided biscuits and sack. "He grew very chearful," Whitgreave recorded "and said, if it would please Almighty God to send him once more an army of ten thousand good and loyall soldiers and subjects, he feared not to expell all those rogues forth of his kingdom." They sat talking for an hour or more until – it must by then have been getting on for four or five in the morning – the King said he would like to lie down on a bed for what remained of the night. Richard Penderel and Francis Yates were then sent back to Boscobel, but John, who had proved such an invaluable courier and had the advantage of being known to Colonel Lane of Bentley, was retained.

The next morning Whitgreave sent all his servants out of the house on various errands or jobs on the estate, with the exception of the kitchen maid who, as a co-religionist, was so far taken into his confidence as to be told that a relation of Father Huddleston's had come to the house for shelter after escaping from Worcester fight. She was, of course, not allowed to see the King (or Wilmot), but this half-explanation would check any embarrassing speculation about the sudden increase in the amount of food she had to prepare. John Penderel was sent over to Bentley to tell Colonel Lane to bring Wilmot's horse to the usual place (a dried marlpit just outside the grounds of Moseley) that night so that the great man could return to Bentley to make the final arrangements for the

[49]

King's journey to Bristol as Jane Lane's mounted servant. What these final arrangements were, or why John Penderel, Colonel Lane and Whitgreave could not see to them themselves without Wilmot's assistance, the evidence does not indicate and imagination cannot easily conjecture. It is hard to believe that they justified the additional risks involved in having Wilmot careering about the countryside yet again. Perhaps the truth is that his mind, as is not uncommon with military men of indifferent abilities, mistook activity for action. The King, who, after all, was still only twenty-one, was too much under his spell to question his wisdom: and Whitgreave and Huddleston, for all their shrewdness and experience, were too much men of their time to question the authority of one who was at once a peer of the realm, a veteran professional officer, and the trusted counsellor of their King.

That still left the above-stairs part of the household to be dealt with, which consisted of Whitgreave's mother (Whitgreave was born in 1618 and had six elder sisters, so she can hardly have been much less than sixty) and Father Huddleston's young pupils. Old Mrs. Whitgreave was taken fully into the secret and introduced to the King, who treated her with his easiest courtesy, insisting that she should sit at table with him at dinner while Whitgreave and Huddleston hovered respectfully behind his chair, serving the food and removing the dishes. The boys were told nothing, but they must have realised that something was in the wind as they were excused lessons and posted at the garret windows with strict orders to report the approach of anyone unusual, especially soldiers. Their preceptor was amused and perhaps a little disconcerted to hear one of them say to the others when they came down to their evening meal: "Eat hard, boys, for we have been on the life-guard and hard duty this day." Soldiers indeed they saw in plenty on this day and the next – but harmless ones; the wretched, starving, ragged survivors of the Scottish infantry begging their way through a

[50]

country that cared nothing for their sufferings. "Humanity after victory", that jewel of Nelson's prayer before the battle of Trafalgar, formed no part of the public policy of the seventeenth century. Even to those who had surrendered the Council of State allowed only a contemptuous pittance, inadequate to maintain bare nourishment, until they were shipped off as slaves to the West Indies. Moseley Hall, it will be remembered, stood close to the public road (hence Whitgreave's refusal to stable Wilmot's horses) and Charles, looking out of the window, recognised among the passers-by a man from his own regiment of Highlanders. Some of them came to the house, where Mrs. Whitgreave gave them food and patched up their wounds as best she could. They told her that they had been living on pea-straw, cabbage stalks and suchlike. All this can hardly have raised the King's spirits or renewed the mood of the night before in which he saw himself at the head of ten thousand stout fellows. To divert his thoughts he gave Whitgreave and Huddleston a long account of what had happened to him in Scotland and described the march to Worcester and the course of the battle there. He inquired about the political loyalties of the neighbouring gentry and sent Whitgreave into Wolverhampton to get intelligence of affairs. Mrs. Whitgreave reported that an old villager had heard that the King, in his retreat, had beaten his enemies at Warrington Bridge and that there were three kings hurrying to his assistance. Charles, amused, remarked: "Surely they are the three kings of Cologne come down from heaven, for I can imagine none else."

The night passed peacefully enough. Colonel Lane collected Wilmot at the appointed hour and it was agreed that they should both return on the following night (Tuesday the 9th) at about the same time to convey Charles to Bentley. Charles again slept fully dressed on his bed while Whitgreave and Huddleston kept watch, one inside and one outside the house. Was it just the routine precaution of thorough and experienced underground activists (they had done nothing of the kind the night before when they had all sat up chatting over sherry and biscuits) or had Whitgreave picked up something in Wolverhampton after all? Extreme danger was, in fact, imminent.

Boscobel and Whiteladies felt the first draught. Either on the Monday or the Tuesday morning they had been subjected to a fairly mild and formal search conducted, it seems, by the local captain to whom Humphrey Penderel had paid the militia money on the Saturday. No doubt he felt he had better clear his yard-arm in case that tiresome Colonel came huffing and puffing back again or, worse still and more likely, put in a report to higher authority. But a few hours later a much graver threat developed. One of the junior officers who had been in the original party that accompanied the King from Worcester had been taken prisoner in Cheshire. His captors, to judge from their subsequent behaviour, were a brutal lot and no doubt their methods of interrogation were uninhibited. Their victim at length disclosed that he had seen the King arrive at Whiteladies early on the Thursday morning after the battle and that he had not seen him leave. In a moment they had him on a horse and set off full gallop for Whiteladies, arriving some hours later in a cloud of dust, their horses blown and lathered. They called for Mr. Giffard and, pressing a pistol against his breast, threatened to shoot him if he did not tell them where the King was. Giffard behaved with courage and dignity, admitting nothing except that a large party of Cavaliers which might or might not have included the King had ridden up to his house early on Thursday morning, had eaten and drunk everything they could find and had then continued their flight northwards. William Penderel and his wife who, poor thing, was much alarmed by the violent behaviour of the soldiers, stuck to the same story. After telling Giffard that they were certainly going to kill him they went into the house and gave it a real going-over, tearing

[52]

up floorboards, breaking down wainscots and looting whatever was portable. When, in the end, they found nothing they turned on their informant and beat him up with the savagery that had characterised all their proceedings.

Fortunately for his peace of mind Whitgreave cannot have heard about this till the following day, as the last thing the Penderels would do would be to risk sending a message to Moseley. The day had begun quietly. Whitgreave joined his mother in the kitchen, leaving Father Huddleston to entertain the King. Charles asked him about the treatment of Roman Catholics under the Parliamentary regime. Huddleston told him that they were now persecuted on account of their loyalty as well as of their religion and offered to show him that, in spite of all, they did not neglect the duties of their Church. He then took him upstairs to see their little chapel. Charles inspected it with reverent curiosity and observed that he had had an altar, crucifix and silver candlesticks of his own until Lord Holland broke them, "which", he added, "he hath now paid for".[1] They then started to turn over Father Huddleston's books, among which Charles singled out a manuscript of Father Huddleston's uncle, *A Short and Plain Way to the Faith and Church*. So short and plain was it that Charles read it through attentively and expressed his complete acceptance of its arguments in terms that would have made Clarendon's hair stand on end. Then he dipped into another work of theological instruction, Turberville's *Catechism*, "said it was a pretty book and that he would take it with him" – a rash intention which, much as it must have pleased his hosts, they would have been far too solicitous of his safety to encourage.

[1] It might with more reason be argued that what this discontented courtier paid for was the luxury of changing sides no less than three times during the course of the Civil War. The narrow vacillation of his life was grimly epitomised by the vote in the Commons that brought him to the block: it was carried by a majority of one.

In the afternoon the King felt drowsy and lay down on his bed. The house was still. Outside nothing broke the peaceful country sounds of a September day. Suddenly Whitgreave, watching at a window, saw a neighbour come running in. A moment later the maid was shouting up the stairs "Soldiers! Soldiers are coming!" This was it. Whitgreave hurried along to the King who, hearing the alarm, was already on his feet. In a minute Whitgreave had secured him in the hiding-place and was ready to deal with the situation. First of all – a master-stroke – he gave orders that all the doors of all the rooms were to be left open. And then, opening the front door and leaving it open behind him, he walked out into the street to meet the search-party.

As soon as they saw him and found out who he was they grabbed him. An ex-Royalist officer, an obstinate recusant, he must obviously have been at Worcester fight: just the sort of trouble-maker they were after. He would have to come along with them. Whitgreave offered no resistance to the rough handling he received, but as soon as he could make himself heard he protested vigorously that he had not been at Worcester or taken any part in the campaign for the very good reason that he had been kept at home by ill-health for a long time past, as any of his neighbours could testify. As a number of these had by this time appeared to see what all the hullabaloo was about, the soldiers could hardly refuse to test the truth of this statement, which, to their great annoyance, was unanimously confirmed. So, after the usual truculent assertions that pass for argument on such occasions, they had to let him go. But he didn't go. He simply continued to stand in the public road in front of his house – and how, exactly, were they to stop him doing that? The provisions of the Road Traffic Act that leap so instantaneously to the modern mind were not ready to hand in the seventeenth century. He stood there, in front of his open door, beyond which other doors stood open, a man with nothing to hide: a man, too, who had already made the soldiers look foolish once. He stood there until he had seen them clear off. And even then he did not go back into the house until he had made sure that they had left the village.

He went straight upstairs and let Charles out of his hole. The King was clearly nervous; Whitgreave seemed to have been away a very long time. But when he heard how everything had turned out he began to be very cheerful again. Fortunately neither of them knew at the time that while the main body of soldiers had been occupied with Whitgreave one of their number had slipped into the yard where the blacksmith was shoeing the horses that had been out to grass for the summer. The soldier questioned the blacksmith and offered him a thousand pounds if he could tell him where the King was. Whether the blacksmith's silence resulted from the strength of his principles or from the thoroughness of Whitgreave's security measures we do not know today.

Later that afternoon Wilmot sent a messenger – almost certainly the long-suffering John Penderel – to confirm that horses would be sent for the King at midnight. Why this needed confirmation, as it had been clearly agreed by all the parties concerned only the night before, is not easy to see. Wilmot, presumably, had nothing to do at Bentley. To occupy himself by sending superfluous messages would flatter his self-importance and disguise the fact that he had no real part to play.

At midnight Colonel Lane arrived at the now familiar rendezvous. Whitgreave met him and led him towards the house, leaving his young nephew Francis Reynolds to hold the horses. Perhaps because he did not care to leave a young boy, unsupported, in charge, the Colonel refused to go beyond the stile leading into the orchard, so Whitgreave returned alone to tell the King that all was ready. Charles immediately asked that Mrs. Whitgreave might be brought to him so that he could take his leave of her. She presented him with some almonds and raisins and other delicacies which she had prepared. The King ate some of them appreciatively and put the rest in his pockets – a less compromising reminder of his friends at Moseley Hall than Turberville's *Catechism*. He thanked them all for the care they had taken of him and promised them that if he came into his own again he would not forget them. They knelt down and said a prayer for his preservation. He then took his leave of Mrs. Whitgreave and gave Whitgreave and Huddleston his hand to kiss. It was time to go.

Leaving Mrs. Whitgreave in the house, they went to meet Colonel Lane, who had now been joined by John Penderel. The King took a grateful farewell of him and accorded him the honour of holding his stirrup while he mounted. The night had turned chilly and rather damp. Father Huddleston pressed him to borrow his cloak, which the King accepted. As he picked up the reins and again expressed his thanks the little party again dropped to their knees, and it was with their prayers to speed him that he followed the hooves of Colonel Lane's horse towards Bentley.

V

A Ride to the West

T HE SHORT journey from Moseley to Bentley divides the
two phases of the King's escape. Up to this point he
had been in acute danger, a hunted man with the hounds
never far behind him. There had been neither time nor means
to frame a plan: it had simply been a question of getting round
the next corner. There was no strategy, except for the vague
intention of making first for Wales and then, when that
proved impracticable, for London. It was all tactics, ex-
pediency, hand-to-mouth measures in which there had been a
considerable element of luck. But, even when this has been
allowed for, there can be no question that the King owed his
preservation to the loyalty, courage and conspiratorial
experience of the Catholic underground. When he left
Moseley he re-entered, under Colonel Lane's tutelage, the
familiar world of Anglican country gentlemen which he had
known all his life and which in all the upheavals of the
seventeenth century retained a consistent and traditional
attachment to Church and King. Such people, by mere force
of habit, maintained some sort of contact with the powers that
be, whatever their political or religious differences. Indeed the
extent of their local influence, and the ramifications of econo-
mic, administrative and, not least, family connexions which
our ancestors succinctly comprehended in the one word
"Interest", made such an accommodation almost inevitable.
Such people disposed, too, of large resources. Shoes, clothes,
food – questions that had hitherto bulked large in Charles's

preoccupations – were questions no longer. Dangers and hardships might – in fact they did – lie in store; but, like those encountered in field sports, they have the air of being appropriate to their background; they were not humiliating and slightly farcical, like being chased up a muddy lane in the middle of the night in shoes that didn't fit. The King was back among people who knew themselves to be the natural masters, not the natural victims, of the State. The change had its compensations as well as its disadvantages.

Bentley itself was simply a staging-post. Charles had a brief conference with Wilmot and Colonel Lane on his arrival in the small hours. It was agreed that he should set out for Abbots Leigh at daybreak and that Wilmot should make his own way there a few days later. He then went to bed. Very early in the morning Colonel Lane came to call him, carrying over his arm a new suit and cloak of grey cloth, such as a tenant farmer's son might wear on a Sunday. This was the identity chosen for him, as it raised less problems than that of a servant. Servants, after all, are generally specialists; and their social life is regulated by a complicated system of customs and conventions, ignorance of which would risk instant exposure. A tenant's son, especially from a distant part of the country, offered a much less distinct conception. After coaching him in the duties of his new capacity, Colonel Lane took Charles to the stables, fitted his stirrups and told him to ride round to the front door. He was mounted on a handsome gelding with a pillion behind his saddle.

Down the steps to meet him came the Colonel's younger sister Jane. She and her cousin Henry Lascelles, who was to ride with them, were the only members of the household to share the secret. She was to be Charles's close companion for many days and to show herself as resourceful as she was attractive. The pictures of her, most of them painted some little time after these adventures, show her good looks and suggest her vitality. Never one to play safe, she is said to have

[58]

answered an inquiry, towards the end of her life, about her testamentary dispositions with the remark that her own hands would be her executors and to have spent everything she could. Two or three letters that Charles wrote her in later years make it plain that he respected as well as liked her. Neither has recorded their first impression of the other, but it is difficult not to believe that Charles must have felt a certain rising of the spirits as he leant from the saddle to give her his arm. Un-acquainted with such everyday matters he offered it the wrong way, a point which old Mrs. Lane, who had got up to see her daughter off, noticed at once. Fortunately Colonel Lane was standing near enough to show him quickly how it ought to be done. It was hardly full daylight and Mrs. Lane might see nothing very extraordinary in the clumsiness of a tenant's son who was probably still half-asleep. Lascelles, Jane's cousin, mounted and, last of all, Jane's sister and brother-in-law, Mr. and Mrs. Petre, who were heading in the direction of Windsor. They of course knew nothing and in any case were to part company from the other three at the end of the first day's journey.

Colonel Lane had arranged that the party should put up for the night at a friend's house in the village of Long Marston, just beyond Stratford-on-Avon. It was a good day's ride of forty miles and more, an exhilarating prospect after the desperate endeavours of the past week which had still not carried the King more than a dozen miles from his first refuge. He was mounted on a good horse and wearing comfortable clothes. They were off to a good start; they knew where they were going; they had a plan. In two days they would be securely based within easy reach of the second largest port in the kingdom. For the first time it really looked as though he was going to bring it off.

As the sun rose it became clear that it was going to be a fine day. Soon after the royal party had left Bentley, Wilmot and Colonel Lane ordered their horses and, taking a hawk and a couple of spaniels with them, announced their intention of visiting Sir Clement Fisher at Packington Hall in Warwickshire for a day's sport. Fisher, who was to marry Jane Lane after the Restoration, was a staunch Royalist and Packington, though lying well to the east of the King's route, would give them a not unplausible pretext for keeping within sight of the royal party for the first few miles. In fact all went well and they were able to see the King well advanced on his journey before they turned their horses' heads towards Sir Clement Fisher's house, where the standards of hospitality were such as Wilmot approved. Under their expansive influence he hit upon the characteristic notion of sending Colonel Lane to London to obtain a pass to go beyond sea in the name of Will Jackson (the name under which the King, in his role of tenant's son, was passing). So off next morning the Colonel went. How hard he tried to execute this commission, of which the probable risks were out of all proportion to the possible use, we do not know. But as nothing came of it and as all his actions show him to have been a man of sense it seems reasonable to infer that, once out of range of his old commanding officer, he used his own discretion.

Getting on towards mid-morning the horse on which the King and Jane were riding cast a shoe. They were approaching Bromsgrove – "a scattering village" as the King remembered it – so, after helping Jane to dismount, he led the horse to the smithy. Nothing could be more ordinary, more everyday, than a man taking a horse to be shod. Yet as Charles walked up to the door of the blacksmith's shop he was making his entrance on the stage in his part as a Staffordshire yeoman. What did one say? What did one do? To any of his subjects the whole proceeding would have been a series of reflex actions. But Charles was not a subject. He had certainly never taken a horse to be shod before in his life. Excellent horseman though he was, he had probably never been taught to put on a saddle and bridle. But he was quick and observant by nature: if he could avoid

[60]

disaster at the outset he would soon be at home in his part. In the event he gave a brilliant performance. His own brief recollection of the scene deserves quoting in full:

"And as I was holding my horse's foot, I asked the smith what news. He told me there was no news that he knew of, since the good news of the beating the rogues of the Scots. I asked him whether there was none of the English taken that joined with the Scots. He answered that he did not hear that that rogue Charles Stuart was taken; but some of the others, he said, were taken, but not Charles Stuart. I told him, that if that rogue were taken he deserved to be hanged, more than all the rest, for bringing in the Scots. Upon which he said that I spoke like an honest man, and so we parted."

Remounting, they made their way towards Stratford, which they had almost reached when suddenly they saw a troop of horse halted about half a mile ahead of them. The soldiers had dismounted and were resting by the roadside, their horses cropping the grass. Charles, whose instinct never failed him in a crisis, saw at once that the safest thing to do was to take no notice and go straight on. He hurriedly whispered as much to Jane Lane, who agreed with him, but unfortunately her brother-in-law, Mr. Petre, would not listen to her. He had been beaten up by Parliamentary soldiers on an earlier occasion and did not wish to repeat the experiment. Very likely they would steal his horse into the bargain. He insisted on turning off the road and approaching Stratford another way. What made it all the more exasperating for Charles was that Stratford was the very point at which Mr. and Mrs. Petre were to part from them. Another mile or two and they could each have pleased themselves. But it was out of the question for a young tenant's son to argue with a gentleman. Feeling every eye drawn to them he obediently turned his horse off the road. After a detour of three or four miles they duly entered Stratford, where whom should they meet but the troop of horse, now mounted and filling the narrow street. This time

[61]

there could be no going back. Even going forward looked difficult enough, but as they came up to them the ranks were opened to let them pass and civil greetings were exchanged. Soon after leaving the town Charles and Jane, accompanied now only by Lascelles, turned south-west for Long Marston, which they reached without further incident.

Their hosts, of course, knew nothing of the identity of Jane's servant, who was sent to the kitchen to help prepare the supper for his betters. The cook, who could no doubt have got on much faster without this tall young man standing politely in the way, asked him to wind up the jack – a cumbrous clockwork machine, even by that date almost obsolescent, for turning joints on the spit. This Charles obediently but unsuccessfully attempted. "What countryman are you," snapped the cook, already hot and flustered, "that you know not how to wind up a jack?" It was a nasty question. With admirable presence of mind Charles supplied the perfect answer: "I am a poor tenant's son of Colonel Lane, in Staffordshire; we seldom have roast meat, but when we have, we don't make use of a jack." The cook, if not soothed, was at least satisfied. This little exchange shows not only how quickly Charles could think but also how quick he was to learn. What had he known, ten days ago, about the dietary of small farmers in Staffordshire? But he had noticed what a rare luxury butcher's meat was to the Penderels and he had remembered.

The next day they pushed on to Cirencester. It was an uneventful journey, so uneventful that not even legend has decorated their route, which presumably lay by Stow-on-the-Wold and Northleach, with picturesque anecdotes and improbable hospitalities. At Cirencester they put up at an inn, Charles sharing a bedroom with Lascelles.

The last day's stage was the shortest but potentially the most dangerous. To reach Abbots Leigh, which lay a few miles to the west of Bristol on the south bank of the Avon, they would have to pass through the city. Apart from the fact that any great port was likely to be closely watched by the authorities, there was the added danger of casual recognition. Charles had been in Bristol for several months during the closing stages of the Civil War and must have been a familiar figure to many. That had been six years ago: he was fifteen then, he was twenty-one now. But the man and the boy were not so very different in appearance, as events were to show. In spite of these risks he could not resist seeing what alterations had been made to the fortifications after the surrender of the place to Parliament and made a detour to look at them. According to one account he lost his way while doing this and had to ask a passer-by for directions. Even so they encountered no trouble and arrived safely at Abbots Leigh late in the afternoon of Friday, September 12th.

Abbots Leigh was the most magnificent of all the houses in which Charles was sheltered during his escape. A drawing made in 1788, only twenty years before it was pulled down, shows a main front of twelve gables, surmounting three storeys of cowled windows; a comfortable, solid west country Elizabethan house. A game of bowls was being played on the lawn beside the drive and a clergyman was sitting on the railings looking on. The Nortons welcomed Jane and Lascelles into the hall, leaving the King to take the horses round to the stables. While Mr. Norton did the honours of the house to Mr. Lascelles, his wife took Jane up to her room for the pleasure of an uninterrupted chat. Jane took advantage of this exchange of intimacies to mention that her servant Will Jackson was only just convalescent from a severe quartan ague – an obsolete ailment which sounds, and probably was, a good deal worse than a sharp attack of influenza whose symptoms it resembled. The poor boy was still looking peaky. "And the truth is," Charles told Pepys in recollecting this passage of his adventures, "my late fatigues and want of meat had indeed made me look a little pale." Would it be asking

[63]

too much if he could be allowed to go straight to bed and have his supper sent up to him? Her hostess entirely understood. She told her that the clergyman she had seen watching the bowls as she arrived was a certain Dr. Gorge who had been turned out of his living by the Parliament and now practised as a physician. Nothing would be easier than to get him to have a look at him.

Charles was indeed thankful not to have to run the social and conversational gauntlet of a large servants' hall in a part of the country where he had been so well known. Even so the solicitude of his hosts did not leave him entirely without anxieties. Pope, the butler, brought him his supper and seemed to take noticeably good care of him. Margaret Rider, Mrs. Norton's maid, brought him a carduus posset, the seventeenth-century equivalent of arrowroot. Last of all, Dr. Gorge came to visit his patient. Darkness had fallen by now and Charles moved over to the side of the bed farthest away from the candle. Dr. Gorge was a local man and an ardent Royalist; the danger of recognition was acute. The Doctor sat down on the bed and took his pulse. He asked several questions which Charles answered briefly and drowsily, making no effort to conceal his desire to be left to go to sleep. Dr. Gorge returned to the drawing-room and reported to Jane, in the best traditions of his adopted profession, "that he had been with William, and that he would do well". His prognosis was correct. After a good night's sleep Charles awoke with a keen appetite or, as he himself put it, "a very good stomach". No doubt it was made all the better for the discovery that his medical attendant had left the house very early in the morning.

The account that Charles gave to Pepys of what transpired at breakfast is so clear and full as to be worth giving at length:

"I . . . went to the buttery hatch to get my breakfast, where I found Pope and two or three other men in the room, and we all fell to eating bread and butter, to which he gave us very good ale and sack. And as I was sitting there, there was one

[64]

that looked like a country fellow sat just by me, who, talking, gave so particular an account of the battle of Worcester to the rest of the company, that I concluded he must be one of Cromwell's soldiers. But I asking him, how he came to give so good an account of that battle? He told me he was in the King's regiment, by which I thought he meant one Colonel King's regiment. But questioning him further, I perceived he had been in my regiment of guards, in Major Broughton's company, that was my major in the battle. I asked him what kind of a man I was? To which he answered by describing exactly both my clothes and my horse; and then looking upon me, he told me that the King was at least three fingers taller than I. Upon which I made what haste I could out of the buttery, for fear he should indeed know me, as being more afraid when I knew he was one of our own soldiers, than when I took him for one of the enemy's.

"So Pope and I went into the hall, and just as we came into it Mrs. Norton was coming by through it; upon which I, plucking off my hat and standing with my hat in my hand as she past by, that Pope looked very earnestly in my face. But I took no notice of it, but put on my hat again, and went away, walking out of the house into the field.

"I had not been out half an hour, but coming back I went up to the chamber where I lay; and just as I came thither Mr. Lascelles came to me, and in a little trouble said, 'What shall we do? I am afraid Pope knows you, for he says very positively to me that it is you, but I have denied it.' Upon which I presently, without more ado, asked him whether he was a very honest man or no. Whereto he answering me, that he knew him to be so honest a fellow that he durst trust him with his life, as having been always on our side, I thought it better to trust him, than go away leaving that suspicion upon him; and thereupon sent for Pope, and told him that I was very glad to meet him there, and would trust him with my life as an old acquaintance. Upon which, being a discreet fellow, he asked

[65]

me what I intended to do; 'for', says he, 'I am extremely happy I know you, for otherwise you might run great danger in this house. For though my master and mistress are good people, yet there are at this time one or two in it that are very great rogues, and I think I can be useful to you in any thing you will command me'."

In fact he proved invaluable. John Pope had been falconer to Sir Thomas Jermyn, one of Charles I's courtiers, before the Civil War and had often seen Charles II as a boy at Richmond. During the way he had served with the King's army. If it was luck that threw him in his way, Charles showed his usual flair in making the most of it. He at once took Pope completely into his confidence, asking him to find out if there were any ships in Bristol bound for French or Spanish ports and telling him that he expected Lord Wilmot to join him at Abbots Leigh that very day. This intelligence greatly alarmed Pope. There were several people in the house who would certainly recognise Wilmot. He would therefore make it his business to intercept him and to arrange for him to be smuggled into the house at night. After that had been attended to he would go into Bristol and make discreet inquiries about sailings for the Continent.

VI

Trent

WILMOT, AS we have seen, believed in doing things in style. He preferred the risks (to others as well as himself) of travelling on horseback to the discomfort and exertion of walking; he could not be bothered with disguises; he regarded the opportunities of sampling the hospitality of the more commodious houses in the country through which he happened to be passing as one of the perquisites of being on the run – if so low a phrase could be applied to a progress that was rarely hurried and never furtive. He had even, it appears, retained the services of his batman, Robert Swan. Swan, who was to play no inconsiderable part in the adventures that lay ahead, is not mentioned by name until after the fugitives had left Bentley Hall. Indeed there are only two direct references to him in the sources for that stage of the affair: ". . . my lord *and his man* were at last brought into the house [Moseley Hall], where Mr. Whitgreave (after some refreshment given them) conveys them into a secret place . . ." and ". . . Lord Willmott (as himself related) apprehending the London road his likelyest way to Escape, took John Penderell to guide him *and his servant* thereinto."[1] Yet all the other sources obliquely but conclusively confirm his presence, because they all mention the problem of accommodating Wilmot's horses, never Wilmot's horse. Why should he need, how could he manage, more than one unless he had somebody with him? At any rate he was attended by

[1] Blount's *Boscobel* and Father Huddleston's *Brief Account*. My italics.

Swan when he met and was of course instantly recognised by Captain Thomas Abington while making his way from Packington to Abbots Leigh. This re-union between old comrades – Abington, like so many Royalists officers, had served for a time under Wilmot – took place at Pinbury Park, a handsome property some few miles west of Cirencester, on the morning of Friday, September 12th, the day on which Charles arrived at Abbots Leigh. Wilmot, no doubt eager to acquire gastronomic intelligence from Abington, who was a Gloucestershire man, seems to have had no hesitation in disclosing his destination. Abington offered to conduct him in person to the seat of Mr. John Winter at Dyrham, a few miles north of Bath, from which it would be but a few hours' ride to Abbots Leigh. Wilmot was happy to accept and, it is to be hoped, was accommodated in the style to which he was accustomed.

The next morning he set off to join the King, accompanied not only by his man, Robert Swan, but by a servant of Winter's called Henry Rogers who was to act as guide. One is only surprised that he did not take Captain Abington along with him to act as A.D.C. Fortunately, as we know, Pope was on the lookout for him and stopped him two or three miles from Abbots Leigh. He then found quarters in a neighbouring village for Wilmot and Robert Swan, and for Henry Rogers, whose services Wilmot thought fit to retain. Having neutralised the immediate threat to the King's security and arranged to bring Wilmot to the house after dark, he went into Bristol to see what he could find out about ships in the port. This proved disappointing. Pope could hear of nothing suitable in less than a month. It was out of the question for the King to remain so long in so dangerous a neighbourhood. Some other way must be found. By the time he collected Wilmot for his secret meeting with the King that night the resourceful Pope had hit on it.

Since Bristol, the principal port of the west, offered no immediate prospect of a passage to the Continent, surely the

[68]

direction to make for was the Channel coast itself. What was wanted was a secure base from which inquiries could be made along a whole stretch of the southern seaboard. These conditions were ideally met in Pope's proposal. Forty miles to the south of Abbots Leigh, on the borders of Somerset and Dorset, lay the little village of Trent. Two or three miles north-west of Sherborne, it was within easy reach of Lyme Regis and Poole, and not more than a day's journey from Portsmouth and Southampton. The manor house there had recently become the property of Colonel Francis Wyndham by his marriage with the heiress Anne Gerard. Did Pope know that the Gerards had been a recusant family and that the house was therefore likely to afford, as indeed it did, the additional security of a priest's hole? Probably not. But he certainly knew that Francis Wyndham would be a good man in a tight corner. He had shewn his initiative in seizing Dunster Castle from the Luttrells in 1643 when they were inclining to the Parliamentary side and his courage and competence in holding it for the King until everyone else had surrendered. He had then obtained good conditions for himself and his troops and had retired into private life.

Charles and Wilmot received the suggestion enthusiastically. Needless to say Colonel Wyndham's military career had included a period of service under Wilmot, so there would be happy memories of mess life to be revived. Charles, too, knew both him and his family well. His elder brother, Edmund, had served right through the war and had followed the King into exile. An even more intimate tie arose from Edmund's having married the daughter of the King's wet-nurse. It was agreed that they should set out on the Tuesday morning, September 16th. Charles would travel, as before, with Lascelles and Jane Lane. Wilmot would go on ahead to give the Wyndhams a few hours' notice of the King's arrival, travelling independently, which meant, of course, attended by Robert Swan and accompanied by Henry Rogers to act as guide. It was like

[69]

Wilmot's usual luck that his recent hostess, Mrs. Winter of Dyrham, should turn out to be a sister of Mrs. Francis Wyndham and that Rogers should therefore be both familiar with the route and well known to the family at Trent.

Everything seemed to fit perfectly. To give Wilmot time to prepare the Wyndhams for the reception of their guest the royal party would put up for the night at Castle Cary, about ten miles from Trent. After seeing the King safely into the hands of his new hosts Jane Lane and Lascelles would return to Bentley.

On the very evening before they were due to leave Abbots Leigh, a cruel stroke upset their plans. Poor Mrs. Norton, after a short labour, gave birth to a still-born child. The shock threw the whole household into disarray. How could Jane Lane, who had made the long expedition from Staffordshire for the express purpose of seeing her friend through the anxieties of childbed, simply clear off the next morning and leave her in the lurch? Now if ever was the reason for her presence. Quite apart from the fact that the Nortons would be deeply, and justly, hurt, so sudden a departure would certainly arouse comment and speculation. On the other hand, the dangers of postponement were great. Wilmot would have to be informed and, presumably, detained in the neighbourhood where his appearance and habits would be sure, sooner rather than later, to attract unwelcome attentions. If Jane were to stay until Ellen Norton's nervous equilibrium was re-established how long might that be? Too much was at stake and the odds already too great to take account of such incalculable elements. Charles himself saw the solution. A letter must arrive that night telling Jane that her father was gravely ill and that she must return to Bentley immediately. Pope delivered it to her at supper and both of them played their parts so well that everybody present believed old Mr. Lane to be at death's door. Of course there was no question but that Jane and her escort must leave first thing the next morning.

[70]

So the rising sun saw them heading towards Bristol and the north. Will Jackson's ague seemed much improved. This time he rode by himself with the portmanteau strapped to his crupper while Jane rode pillion to Lascelles. As soon as they were well clear of Abbots Leigh they turned south and, after an uneventful ride through thinly populated country, arrived safely at Castle Cary. They were met outside the town by Edward Kirton, the steward of the old Marquis of Hertford who had been Charles's tutor, who had made arrangements for their reception. He knew Wilmot well and had recognised him on his way through the place a few hours earlier. That explains how he knew the King was coming. Perhaps it also explains Charles's remark to Pepys at this point in his narrative: ". . . my Lord Wilmot . . . whom I still took care not to keep with me, but sent him a little before, or left to come after me." To which he subsequently added, "I could never get my Lord Wilmot to put on any disguise, he saying that he should look frightfully in it, and therefore did never put on any".

That Charles was not alone in thinking that Wilmot carried his whims in this matter a little far is confirmed by the account of his Lordship's arrival at Trent that same evening. Henry Rogers went into the house while Wilmot and Robert Swan waited outside. The account, which was written by Anne Wyndham, the Colonel's wife, runs as follows:

"Rogers was sent in forthwith to the Colonel, to acquaint him that a gentleman, a friend of his, desired the favour of him that he would please to step forth and speak with him. The Colonel enquiring of Rogers whether he knew the gentleman or his business, [he] answered no; he understood nothing at all, but only that he was called by the name of Mr. Morton. Then, without further discourse, the Colonel came forth, and found the gentleman walking near the stable, whom, as soon as he approached (although it was somewhat dark) he saluted by the title of my Lord Wilmot. His Lordship seemed to wonder that he should be known; but it was nothing strange, considering the Colonel's former acquaintance with him, being one of the first that engaged under his command in his late majesty's service; besides his Lordship was not in the least altered, except a hawk on his fist, and a lure by his side, might pass for a disguise. This confidence of his Lordship really begat admiration[1] in the Colonel, calling to mind the great danger he was in, and whose harbinger he was; for he advertised the Colonel that the King himself was on his way to Trent, intending that very night to lodge at Castle Cary . . . hoping by God's assistance to be with him about ten of the clock next morning.''

The Colonel was overjoyed, as he had heard that the King had been killed at the Battle of Worcester – another instance of the slow and inaccurate dissemination of news that was one of the elements in the situation entirely favourable to Charles. No anti-feminist, he at once took into his confidence his wife, his mother, his mother's niece Julian Coningsby, two female domestics and one manservant, Henry Peters. To a modern ear this sounds almost like a census return, but we know from Anne Wyndham herself that the whole household consisted of no less than twenty-six persons, and this figure would probably not include children. Arrangements were quickly made to find jobs for those who were not in the secret which would keep them out of the way at the time at which the King was expected, and rooms were chosen for him that would allow easy access to the priest's hole.

Between nine and ten the next morning, when everybody had been sent about their business, the Colonel and his wife went out for a stroll in the fields adjoining the house. Sure enough they soon saw the little party approaching. Charles was riding on the double gelding with Jane. As soon as they were

[1] In the seventeenth century this word still retained its classical meaning of wonder or astonishment. The Colonel found Wilmot's attitude incredible rather than commendable.

within earshot he called out to the Colonel, "Frank, Frank, how dost thou do?" The relief at finding himself once more among familiar friends after the nightmare of the last fortnight was like a foretaste of escape. The Penderels and Pope the butler, Whitgreave and Huddleston and Colonel Lane, all had been staunch friends and most considerate hosts. But he had never met any of them before: it had been impossible to relax, to feel at home, to gossip about mutual acquaintances and thus to forget for a few minutes the necessity that had brought him to their door. For all his apparent maturity he was only twenty-one. The Colonel had tears in his eyes as he led him into the house.

As soon as the first introductions were over Wilmot was brought in and the ladies withdrew. It was agreed that Jane Lane should be entertained as a relation of the family and that she and Lascelles should start for home the next morning. Colonel Wyndham, who was still much moved, then told the King and Wilmot of a scene that had taken place shortly before the death of his own father, Sir Thomas Wyndham, in 1636. The old man, feeling that he had not long to live, summoned all his five sons whom he had not seen together for some years and spoke to them in solemn terms of the blessings of peace and prosperity that the country had enjoyed under its last three monarchs, and contrasted them with the calamities of foreign invasion and internal conflict that so many of their forebears had had to endure.

"He mentioned the healing conjunction of the two houses of York and Lancaster, and the blessed union of the two crowns of England and Scotland, stopping up those fountains of blood which, by national feuds and quarrels kept open, had like to have drowned the whole island. He said he feared the beautiful garment of peace would shortly be torn in pieces through the neglect of the magistrates, the general corruption of manners, and the prevalence of a puritanical faction, which (if not prevented) would undermine the very pillars of government.

[73]

'My sons! we have hitherto seen serene and quiet times, but now prepare yourselves for cloudy and troublesome. I command you to honour and obey our gracious sovereign, and in all times to adhere to the crown; and though the crown should hang upon a bush, I charge you forsake it not'."

On this dramatic line the old man had risen from his chair and left them, impressed but somewhat mystified by his allusion to the crown hanging upon a bush. It seems that they had not inherited his knowledge of English history. However, the words stuck in their minds; and recent events had removed any doubts as to their meaning or their aptness.

From this personal, but not irrelevant, digression they turned to the question of finding a ship. Colonel Wyndham pointed out that Melbury Court, the seat of the Strangways family, lay only ten miles to the south over the county boundary. The Strangways were great people in Dorset and, among their extensive financial interests, were quite certain to have connexions in the coastal trade; they might even own a vessel or two themselves. Old Sir John Strangways, an ardent Royalist, was still alive, and his two sons, both of whom had held colonelcies in the King's army, were living in the house. If the King and Wilmot agreed he would ride over next day and see if they could help. Charles at once approved the suggestion. So next morning, after Jane Lane and Lascelles had said goodbye, the Colonel set off for Melbury. On his arrival he was met by one of the sons, Colonel Giles Strangways. Wyndham dismounted and the two men strolled into the park. Giles Strangways listened sympathetically but said that, to his great regret, he could do nothing about obtaining a passage for the King. He and his family had indeed had a number of friends and acquaintances amongst merchants and skippers but these had all been to do with ships sailing from Weymouth, and all the trustworthy people there had, because of their previous Royalist activities, either been banished or had found it advisable to banish themselves. In Poole and Lyme he was a total stranger. He only wished he could be of service and as a token of his loyalty sent the King a hundred pounds in gold, which was all the ready money he had by him. Wyndham accepted his protestations and his cash and returned to Trent. If he felt that the leading Royalist family of North Dorset might have exerted themselves rather more in the supreme crisis of their cause he did not say so. It was the first, but it was certainly not the last, instance of Royalist ardour proving a little tepid when it came to the touch. Two disastrous civil wars followed by the Scottish fiasco just ended had had a cooling effect on those who had great possessions. The grandees of the King's party played a noticeably small part in his escape.

Back at Trent Wyndham reported his lack of success and handed over the money to Wilmot. On his journey to the coast, whenever that took place, Charles would still retain the character of a mounted servant. Such a man would never have more than a few shillings in his pocket. Wyndham now thought of two merchants in Lyme whom he had heard of as having Royalist sympathies, Captain Alford and Captain Ellesdon. Accordingly the following day he went to call on them. Alford turned out to be away in Portugal on a voyage, but Ellesdon, whose captaincy seems to have derived from his service in the Royalist army rather than on the quarter-deck of a ship, was at home. Politically he was not quite of the antecedents Wyndham would have preferred as, in spite of his own record of service in the war, he had recently married a rich widow of strict Presbyterian views. In the alarming events that followed it was freely asserted by some of those concerned that Ellesdon had been playing a double game, but Clarendon, who investigated these allegations after the Restoration, was convinced that there was nothing in them. Anyhow, he at once welcomed Wyndham's suggestion that he might help to spirit a couple of Royalist fugitives across the Channel. Sending to the Custom House to inquire what ships were entered as bound for France, he found that one of his own tenants, a certain

[75]

Stephen Limbry, had certified his intention of taking his small coasting vessel over to St. Malo early in the following week. This was a real piece of luck. Consulting with Wyndham, Ellesdon cooked up a story about two merchants whose creditors were about to foreclose but who had certain debts owed to them in France which they could only collect by going over in person. Armed with this fiction they both rode over to the neighbouring village of Charmouth, where Limbry lived, and got him to agree to take them for a fee of £60, payable on his return to Lyme. There is a conflict of evidence as to how much both Ellesdon and Limbry actually knew. It seems probable that Wyndham originally told Ellesdon that he was trying to find a passage for Wilmot and a servant, and that the same half-truth was offered to Limbry, with the cover story about the merchants to provide him with answers to any awkward questions he might be asked by his crew. Whatever precautions were in fact taken it was not long before everyone concerned knew very well who was really involved.

This conversation took place on Friday, September 19th. Limbry's ship was lying inside the cob at Lyme. He would have to ballast her and then warp her out of the harbour. This he would do the following Monday, the 22nd, and then after dark sail along the coast to Charmouth, where he would send his longboat to pick up his passengers from the beach about midnight. If the wind was favourable they would be out of sight of the coast before dawn. The tide made it impossible to sail earlier.

Wyndham was anxious to get back to Trent with the good news as fast as he could, but he did not allow his excitement to carry him away. How was the King's final approach to be made? His first idea was that the royal party should come to Lyme during daylight and should set out for Charmouth beach after dark. Ellesdon, who had at first approved the plan, remembered that there would be a fair in Lyme that Monday.

The town would be packed with people, and though as a general rule there was safety in numbers the recent proclamation of the reward for the King's capture, a proclamation which was likely to be repeated on the day of the fair, might stimulate undesirable curiosity. The inn at Charmouth where they had held their conference with Limbry was the obvious place to wait. But here there were two points to be attended to. First, accommodation ought to be reserved in case the inn should be filled with fairgoers who had not managed to find a bed in Lyme. And second, some explanation must be given for the guests departing in the middle of the night. They agreed that the best expedient would be to send Wyndham's servant, Henry Peters, to book the rooms next day. Over a glass of wine he could then tell the hostess a romantic story of elopement that would engage her sympathy and quiet both her suspicions and her tongue. Peters's master, a young man of family and fortune, was in love with a beautiful young woman who returned his passion and was in every way suited to marry him. Her relations, however, were unalterably opposed to the marriage, which in consequence would have to take place secretly. The prospective bride and groom would arrive at Charmouth on Monday evening, but in view of the danger of pursuit they would not dare to go to bed and might have to leave at any moment. Wyndham's cousin, Julian Coningsby, was the young lady; Charles her manservant; and Wilmot the bridegroom.

The story, for Henry Peters called at the inn the next day, went down admirably. How could any right-minded hostess resist such a tale, especially when substantiated by payment in advance? The final details of the adventure were settled as Ellesdon accompanied Wyndham on the first few miles of his ride back to Trent. They were not to meet again till a few hours before the King's embarkation. While Wyndham would be responsible for getting the King to Charmouth and for arrangements at the inn, Ellesdon would keep in touch with

Limbry and see that he performed his part of the bargain. Just in case anything went wrong on either side they agreed to a general rendezvous at an isolated farm belonging to the Ellesdon family in the hills some three or four miles from the coast. So that there could be no mistake Ellesdon took Wyndham to see it. There they parted and the Colonel rode back to Trent.

Charles and Wilmot approved the scheme wholeheartedly, as well they might. It was one thing to dodge about the countryside evading capture: it was quite another, as they had learned at Abbots Leigh, to find a ship. And now Frank Wyndham had cleared this stiffest of hurdles within two days of receiving them into his house. Another three days and they would be clear away. The King's pleasure and excitement were the keener because he seems to have found Trent, though he was too polite to say so, dreadfully dull. The house was so close to the village and so full of people that he could not leave his room. Safe and secure he might be, compared with Boscobel or Moseley, but one couldn't take a book into the garden. And the Wyndhams, admirable people, excellent hosts, were Royalists of a familiar type; there were no intellectual excursions into the forbidden territory of Roman Catholicism; there were not even, it seems, many books. Charles whiled away the time cooking his own meals and boring holes through gold coins, some of which he later presented to the people who helped him to escape.

There had been one mild excitement during the Colonel's absence. Suddenly in the middle of the morning there had been a great to-do in the village. Bonfires had been lit and the church bells had been rung. Charles sent one of the two maids who knew of his presence to inquire what it was all about. She came back a few minutes later to tell him that a Parliamentary trooper had appeared in the village claiming that he personally had killed the King and that the buff coat he was wearing had been stripped from the corpse. There was no denying the

[78]

spontaneity of the enthusiasm with which the news had been received. From his window he could see the joyful crowd gathering in the churchyard. "Alas! poor people," he said.

Certainly the villagers of Trent seem to have been a headstrong, moody, murmuring race. Early on Sunday morning the village tailor warned Colonel Wyndham that it was rumoured that there were persons of quality hidden in the manor and that it was planned to search the house and seize them. Needless to say Wilmot was to thank for this last-minute threat to the whole enterprise, as Anne Wyndham's account makes clear:

"The Colonel (rewarding the good man for his care and kindness towards himself and his family) told him that his kinsman (meaning the Lord Wilmot) was not private but public in his house (for so his lordship pleased to be) and that he believed he would show himself in the church at the time of prayers. When the honest fellow was gone, the Colonel acquaints the King what passed between himself and the tailor, and withal besought his majesty to persuade the Lord Wilmot to accompany him to church, thinking, by this means, not only to lessen the jealousy, but also to gain the good opinion of some of the fanaticks, who would be apt to believe that the Colonel was rather brought to church by my lord than his lordship by the Colonel, who seldom came to that place since faction and rebellion had justled out and kept possession against peace and religion. He alleged, moreover, that he sate in an aisle distinct from the body of the congregation, so that the parishioners could not take a full view of any of his company. These reasons, joined with his majesty's command, prevailed with his lordship; and (though he thought it a bold adventure, yet) it not only allayed the fury but also took out the very sting of those wasps, insomuch that they, who the last night talked of nothing but searching, began now to say that Cromwell's late success against the King had made the Colonel a convert."

It was fitting that the disregard of security precautions should be punished by the infliction of an extra church parade.

VII

Fiasco

ON MONDAY morning the King set out from Trent. He was only a few hours' ride from the coast, and that was easy country – no towns, no patrols, no guarded bridges. He was a long way from Worcester and there had been no sign that anyone had picked up his track. After dark a ship would be waiting; a deserted beach, the longboat softly grounding on the sand. Could it really be so simple? He had resumed his character of a mounted servant and Julian Coningsby was riding pillion. Her cousin Colonel Wyndham rode with them to act as guide. A little way behind, so as not to seem to form part of the same expedition, rode Wilmot accompanied by Wyndham's man, Henry Peters. Robert Swan was left behind at Trent. Had the King, perhaps, put his foot down?

They reached the farm up in the hills in the late afternoon and found Ellesdon waiting for them. He had told the tenant that he was expecting two or three friends who were travelling down with the London carrier, and he at once welcomed them into the house. In spite of the remote situation it does not seem to have been an ideal rendezvous. The tenant is said to have been a strong Cromwellian and there is even a story that he recognised the King and went off to consult a neighbour as to whether it would be right to report his presence to the authorities. The neighbour, who is the reputed source of this anecdote, persuaded him not to, telling him that "as he was come for safety under his roof, he should in nowise betray

him but let him go as he came; it would be the price of blood
and it would do no good''. Fortunately for his peace of mind
Ellesdon was unaware of this interesting case of conscience, if
indeed it ever arose at all. He told Charles that he had seen
Limbry that morning and that everything was going according
to plan. Limbry would be in Charmouth that evening and
would call at the inn to see Colonel Wyndham and confirm
final arrangements. Divine approval was manifest in a steady
offshore breeze which gave every sign of holding through the
night. Charles thanked Ellesdon profusely, promised to grant
him any reward within reason after he was restored to his
throne, and gave him a gold coin with a hole through the
middle to be going on with. Everybody then remounted and
set off towards Lyme. When they were out of sight of the farm
the royal party left Ellesdon to continue his journey alone and
turned south-east for Charmouth.

They arrived at the inn shortly after sunset. Henry Peters's
story of the runaway marriage assured them a conspiratorial
welcome from the proprietress. Wilmot and Julian Coningsby,
squired by Charles, at once retired to the room reserved for
them, while Wyndham and Peters hung about downstairs,
ostensibly to give the alarm if Julian's relations should appear
in pursuit, but really to keep a look-out for Limbry. He
appeared about an hour after their arrival and confirmed that
all was well. The longboat would come to fetch them off
about midnight. He was going straight from the inn to his
house to collect his things and would be on board in good
time.

Four hours to go. Charles and Wilmot and Julian Coningsby
had supper in their room and sat waiting. Wyndham and
Peters ate downstairs. At last, when it was well past eleven,
they slipped out and went down to the beach. As soon as the
boat was sighted one of them would pass the word to the two
men, who must have felt that half their life had been spent in
the Queen's Arms at Charmouth. The minutes passed and

congealed into hours. Midnight was long gone and nothing broke the unchanging pattern of sounds: the thump of the breakers tumbling on the steep beach followed by the swish of little stones sucked back by the receding water, the wind, that tantalising wind, singing in their ears. Over the sea the darkness began to pale into the half-light that makes way for dawn. Resignation, anxiety, disappointment, frustration were swept away by a sudden sense of acute danger. No boat could come now. Something had gone gravely wrong. The King must be got away at once.

Wyndham's urgency at once convinced the King, but Wilmot was full of objections. They had a ship, hadn't they? If there had been some hitch they could always try again the following night. Where were they to go to, anyway? He was in favour of staying put.

At last a compromise was reached. Charles, accompanied by Julian Coningsby and Wyndham, was to set out at once along the London road. When they got to Bridport, about five miles away, they would take a room at the principal inn and wait for Wilmot and Peters, who would meanwhile find out what Limbry had been playing at. If it were simply some minor and easily remediable difficulty the whole party could then return to Charmouth that evening. If it meant abandoning the whole idea, the sooner they were right away the better.

The sun was well up by the time they mounted and there were plenty of travellers on the London road. Among those coming towards Lyme Charles and Wyndham suddenly recognised an old servant of Charles I. They saw from his eyes that he recognised them, but to their relief he gave no sign of having done so. As they approached Bridport they saw that the whole place was alive with soldiers. Colonel Haines's regiment was amongst the forces the Government were concentrating in the south-western ports for the reduction of Jersey, the last Royalist stronghold and base for Rupert's fleet. At the sight of the redcoats Colonel Wyndham, who had been through a very trying twenty-four hours, momentarily lost his nerve. He begged the King at all costs to avoid the town. As on the similar occasion at Stratford, Charles saw at once that boldness was the safest and the wisest policy. And this time he was in a position to be adamant. Brushing aside the Colonel's fears he rode coolly into the town and up to the best inn. How else, he pointed out to Wyndham, could they be sure of regaining contact with Wilmot? And the thought of that magnifico caracoling about the countryside in search of them must have brought the Colonel up with a round turn.

What followed is best described in the King's own account: "We found the yard very full of soldiers. I alighted, and taking the horses thought it the best way to go blundering in amongst them, and lead them through the middle of the soldiers into the stable; which I did, and they were very angry with me for my rudeness.

"As soon as I came into the stable I took the bridle off the horses, and called the hostler to me to help me, and to give the horses some oats. And as the hostler was helping me to feed the horses, 'Sure, Sir,' says the hostler, 'I know your face?' which was no very pleasant question to me. But I thought the best way was to ask him, where he had lived? Whether he had always lived there or no? He told me that he was but newly come thither; that he was born in Exeter, and had been hostler in an inn there, hard by one Mr. Potter's, a merchant in whose house I had lain in the time of war: so I thought it best to give the fellow no further occasion of thinking where he had seen me, for fear he should guess right at last; therefore I told him, 'Friend, certainly you have seen me then at Mr. Potter's, for I served him a good while, above a year'. 'Oh!' says he, 'then I remember you a boy there,' and with that was put off from thinking any more on it; but desired that we might drink a pot of beer together; which I excused by saying that I must go wait on my master, and get his dinner ready for him. But told him that my master was going for London,

[83]

and would return about three weeks hence, when he would lie there, and I would not fail to drink a pot with him.''

While Charles was displaying such enviable coolness and quickness of wit – and it ought to be remembered that he had had no sleep the night before; indeed had spent it in the most exhausting manner imaginable, expecting a summons to crucial action at any minute – Colonel Wyndham was trying to secure a room. After about half an hour he succeeded and even arranged for some roast mutton to be sent up, no mean feat when the place was swarming with hungry, thirsty and well-paid soldiers. The King joined him and while they made a hurried meal Julian Coningsby stood by the window looking out on the inn yard. Suddenly she saw Henry Peters ride in. She signalled to him and a few minutes later he found his way to their room. Wilmot, it appeared, had uncharacteristically misjudged which was the best inn and had gone to another. Finding no sign of the royal party he had sent Peters round with a message to meet him a mile or two outside the town on the London road. As the horses had not been unsaddled they were on their way in a moment and almost immediately they had left Bridport they found Wilmot waiting for them.

What had gone wrong at Charmouth? As soon as the King had left that morning Wilmot had sent Henry Peters into Lyme to find Captain Ellesdon. He, congratulating himself on the King's being halfway across the Channel, was flabbergasted to hear that he was still hiding on the coast. His first thought was that all Limbry's seamen had got dead drunk at the fair, but he soon found out that the real reason was even more embarrassing for the poor man. When Limbry left the Queen's Arms the night before, he went, as he said he would, straight home and told his wife to get his sea-chest ready as he was sailing on the next tide. This was the first that Mrs. Limbry had heard of it: she asked him how he had so suddenly come by a freight. He then admitted that he hadn't, but that their landlord had given him some money and promised him a lot

[84]

more if he would oblige him by taking a couple of gentlemen over to France on the quiet. At this Mrs. Limbry flew into a passion. She had been at Lyme fair that morning and had heard the public proclamation of the rewards and penalties laid down by the Government in connexion with the King's escape. Clearly these people were Royalists; one of them might even be the King himself. Realising from this tirade that he would have to do his own packing, Limbry went into the bedroom to collect his clothes, whereupon his wife shut the door and locked him in, declaring that she was not going to be left a widow and their two daughters fatherless "for ever a landlord of them all". The enraged Limbry hammered at the door, threatening to break it down if she didn't let him out at once. His wife, however, knew a trick worth two of that. Raising her voice, she told him in bell-like tones that if he didn't stay quietly where he was she would scream the place down and bring the neighbours in. Poor Limbry! Any hero of fiction would have wriggled out of this absurd captivity in half a dozen paragraphs. But in spite of the strong suggestion of *opéra bouffe* this was real life. And what *was* he to do? Very sensibly, he did nothing.

The next morning, while Peters was away in Lyme conferring with Ellesdon, Wilmot, tired of waiting, took a stroll through Charmouth to meet him. Gradually he became aware of a man with a crestfallen, imploring expression who seemed to be following him but who was himself dogged by a woman and two girls whose presence was evidently an embarrassment to him. It flashed on Wilmot that this must be the seaman who had let them down and that he wanted to explain what had happened.[1] Although Limbry's domestic circumstances were

[1] Ellesdon, who is the authority for this story, says that it was Wyndham, not Wilmot, who was followed by Limbry. But Wyndham and Limbry must have known each other by sight: they had met and conversed twice, the second time only the evening before. And if, as he hurried up from the beach to the inn, Wyndham had believed himself to be followed by the man he

unknown to him he guessed pretty easily what had upset the plan. In this he had for the moment the advantage of Ellesdon, who, at his wits' end to understand what had gone wrong, sent Peters back to Charmouth with urgent instructions that the royal party should leave the district at once. Wilmot and Peters therefore followed Charles to Bridport and successfully rejoined him, as we have seen.

But, unknown to them all, a far graver danger threatened. It all started with the ostler of the Queen's Arms at Charmouth. He was, in fact, a soldier belonging to the company quartered in the neighbourhood who was supplementing his pay by helping in the inn stables. The nocturnal rambles of Peters and Colonel Wyndham had not escaped his notice: he had also observed the instant readiness for departure maintained by the lady and the two gentlemen who were escorting her. He leapt to the conclusion that the King was making his escape disguised as a woman, a ruse with which Charles was popularly credited, perhaps because everyone knew that his build was tall and slender. He immediately confided his suspicions to his employer, but she, preferring to accept the romantic story she had been told, either because she believed it or because she happened to be a strong Royalist, snubbed him in no uncertain fashion. The next morning, after Charles and Wyndham had set off for Bridport and Peters had gone into Lyme to find Ellesdon, Wilmot discovered that his horse had cast a shoe and told the ostler to have a new one put on at once. As soon as the smith had looked at the horse's feet he remarked that the three remaining shoes had been set in three different counties and

---

had been waiting for all night he would hardly have kept the information to himself. Wilmot, on the other hand, had nothing to do in Charmouth whilst Peters was away in Lyme and it would have been very much in character for him to run the unnecessary risk involved in sauntering about the village while his horse was being shod. Finally, it is improbable that Anne Wyndham would not have mentioned the incident in her extremely detailed account of her husband's part in the affair.

one of them in Worcestershire. As far as the ostler was concerned that clinched it. He poured out all his suspicions to the smith, who listened eagerly and suggested that his best course was to go at once to the parson, who was a notably zealous supporter of the Government. Off hurried the ostler, but the parson, not less conscientious in his religious than his political duties, was at prayer and must on no account be disturbed. Impatiently the ostler waited: on and on went the parson's devotions. Not for nothing was his name Benjamin Westley; his great-grandson John Wesley[1] was to re-animate the religion of his countrymen in the next century. Great as was the ostler's sense of patriotic duty, glittering as must have been the thousand pounds reward, there was just the little matter of Wilmot's tip. The smith would not take more than a few minutes to shoe the horse, and if the ostler were not there when Wilmot wanted to be off he could whistle for his money. No doubt in some agony of mind the ostler opted for the modest but certain rewards of his professional services. The horse was indeed ready; Peters had returned from Lyme; and as soon as he had adjusted matters with the smith and the ostler Wilmot mounted and cantered off towards Bridport.

Back to the parsonage sped the ostler, with the smith clattering behind him. Mr. Westley had at last risen from his knees and was ready to give his undivided attention to the affairs of this world. Excitable and enthusiastic, he hardly waited for them to finish before he was rushing down the street to the Queen's Arms to question its proprietress with, as one account admirably puts it, "most eager Blatterations". He met with a decidedly chilly reception. Jocularity provoked even less happy reactions, as the following exchange shows:

" 'Why how now, Margaret? you are a maid of honour now.' 'What mean you by that, Mr. Parson?' quoth she. Said he 'Why Charles Stuart lay last night at your house, and

[1] The "t" seems to have dropped out of the surname in the lifetime of Benjamin's son, John.

[87]

kissed you at his departure; so that now you can't but be a maid of honour.' The woman began then to be very angry, and told him he was a scurvy-conditioned man to go about to bring her and her house into trouble. 'But,' said she, 'if I thought it was the King, as you say it was, I would think the better of my lips all the days of my life; and so, Mr. Parson, get you out of my house, or else I'll get those shall kick you out.' "

Foiled at the inn, Westley went straight to the nearest Justice of the Peace. But here again he was out of luck. The gentleman in question thought it most improbable that the King should be in that part of the country and, frightened of making an ass of himself, refused to take any action. This second rebuff quenched Westley's enthusiasm: he seems to have dropped the subject with the same rapidity with which he had taken it up. No doubt he had other matters to attend to, as had the blacksmith. But the ostler's blood was up. He suddenly remembered his other career, that of a soldier in the Parliament's army, and reported to his commanding officer, Captain Macy. Why had he neglected to take so obvious a step in the first place? Perhaps his experience of military life had warned him that his share of any official reward was likely, on the analogy of prize money in the navy, to be a precious small one. By informing the civil authorities he stood a good chance of scooping the pool.

At all events he had, at last, come to the right man. Captain Macy listened to his story, called for his horse and a few men to accompany him, and set off for Bridport at the gallop. He entered the town only a few minutes after Charles had left it and lost little time in picking up his trail. Had the King and Wilmot pursued their original plan of pressing on along the main road to Dorchester and London they would certainly have been caught. Luckily for them they decided on the spur of the moment to make for Trent again and try for another ship or even, as they had not yet heard exactly how the original project had misfired, to have another shot at taking passage

[88]

with Limbry. As none of them, not even Wyndham or Peters, knew that part of the country, they thought the best plan would be to take the first turning to the left and head up into the hills in a generally northerly direction. Macy can hardly have missed them by more than five minutes as he thundered past the opening of this insignificant track on his way to Dorchester. Contemporaries were not slow to identify the Divine Hand in this well-timed alteration of course, and latter-day Cavaliers of the Edwardian period have celebrated it in mounted historical pageants and have commemorated what they are pleased to call the Miraculous Divergence by a squat stone monument. Perhaps the best comment on the whole episode was Benjamin Westley's remark "that he was confident that if ever the King did come in again, he would love long prayers; for had he not been then longer than ordinary at his devotions, he had surely snapt him" – pleasant evidence that he shared his great-grandson's sense of humour as well as his graver qualities.

Captain Macy made a thorough search of the inns and ale-houses of Dorchester before returning in no sunny mood to Lyme. He had lost the scent. But he was still convinced that the King could not be far away and he meant to find him. He searched several houses belonging to known Royalists in the neighbourhood, one of them, at Pilsdon, the home of Colonel Wyndham's uncle, Sir Hugh Wyndham. "They took the old baronet, his lady, daughters and whole family, and set a guard upon them in the hall, whilst they examine every corner, not sparing either trunk or box. Then taking a particular view of their prisoners, they seize a lovely young lady, saying she was the King disguised in woman's apparel. At length, being convinced of their rude and gross mistake, they desisted from offering any further violence to that family."

This incident, here described by Anne Wyndham and confirmed by two other accounts, raises two or three points of some interest. It shows, once again, how obsessed people were with the rumour that Charles was making his escape disguised as a woman. And it throws a somewhat strange light on the conduct of Captain Ellesdon. According to Captain Alford, the Royalist skipper whom Colonel Wyndham first tried to get in touch with and whose absence on a voyage to Portugal led to his approaching Ellesdon instead, Captain Ellesdon had appeared at Pilsdon shortly before Macy and his troopers. "He went in boldly and asked Sir Hugh Wyndham for the King. Sir Hugh replied to him that he was a base fellow to come to his house to ask for the King and commanded him out of the house."

How reliable is Captain Alford? At first sight, not very. He was out of the country at the time of the events he describes; his account is violently hostile to Ellesdon throughout; indeed he attributes the failure of the Limbry venture entirely to Ellesdon's bad faith in keeping back the money he had promised to advance him for getting his ship ready for sea. His assertions on this matter are clear and emphatic: but we know from overwhelming evidence, including that of Limbry himself, that they are simply untrue. Why then should we bother any further with Captain Alford's account of the Pilsdon episode? For two good reasons. First, he cites by name two witnesses then living, one of them the man who subsequently married Julian Coningsby and the other, accosted by Ellesdon on that very afternoon just outside Lyme, "whom he desired to go with him, telling him that there was £1,000 to be got for whoever should take the King, and he knew where he was". Second, and even more damaging, Anne Wyndham in her account already quoted provides specific and independent confirmation. "And here it is much to be observed that, the same day the King went from Charmouth, Captain Ellesdon came to Pilisdon, and enquired of Sir Hugh and his lady for the King and Colonel, confidently affirming that they must needs be there." The fact of Ellesdon's visit thus seems established beyond reasonable doubt. But what was his motive? Alford's contention that he had been a traitor from the start is easily dismissed. No one was in a better position to have handed the King over on the Monday afternoon or evening had he wished to do so. But when the plan miscarried, when he heard that Macy and his men were hard on the King's heels, did he begin to think about hedging his bets? If the King were caught the whole story would come out; too many people were involved for there to be any hope of keeping it secret. Might it not be prudent to anticipate this danger by lending a hand in catching him? The alternative explanations favourable to Ellesdon are that he was trying to re-establish contact with the King and Wyndham (but if so, why?) or that he was deliberately leading the pursuit off on a wild-goose chase. Both look pretty thin. And if either had been true he would hardly have omitted the point in his long, entertaining and minutely detailed letter to Clarendon written after the Restoration when he, along with many others, was anxious that the Keeper of the Royal Memory should be reminded of services rendered and promises made. In fact he makes no mention of Pilsdon at all. In the end Ellesdon was among those rewarded for helping the King to escape. And Colonel Wyndham, whose wife's account, quoted above, clearly implied double-dealing, supported his claims with a categorical assertion of his honesty. Clarendon evidently went into the matter with care and was in a better position to find out the truth than anyone else. But on the facts as known to us the question of Ellesdon's conduct remains baffling.

Had Captain Macy but known it his visit to Pilsdon had brought him within two or three miles of the fugitives. Hidden behind the hill called Pilsdon Pen lies the village of Broadwindsor, where Charles and his friends had arrived an hour or two earlier. They were, it seems, thoroughly lost and had halted outside the village inn while Colonel Wyndham went in to inquire the name of the place. By astonishing luck the landlord turned out to be a staunch Royalist whom Wyndham had known slightly some years earlier. Wyndham told him that he and his brother-in-law, Colonel Bullen Reymes (to whom Wilmot bore so striking a resemblance that the landlord's wife, who knew Colonel Reymes, greeted him without introduction as an old acquaintance), had broken their parole by being more than five miles from home. They therefore wished to be given accommodation for the night which would secure them from observation. The landlord obligingly put them in the top storey of the house and served their supper himself. Rooms at the top of inns are never the most comfortable, but the prospects for a peaceful night in this steep and remote village looked decidedly hopeful. But if the Dorset countryside slept, the Commonwealth Government did not. Jersey was still to be reduced: and about nine o'clock a detachment of Colonel Haines's regiment marching to the coast arrived in the village and demanded billets. All the empty rooms in the inn were at once requisitioned, so that the royal party were in effect cut off on the top floor. The noise and confusion of the soldiers settling in made sleep unthinkable. Just as it was beginning to subside one of the women campfollowers went into labour on the kitchen floor and, somewhere in the small hours, was delivered of a child. The hubbub and excitement attendant on these proceedings awoke the whole village; awoke it, too, to the horrid probability that the military would clear off next morning leaving the child on the parish. To avert this financial calamity the leading inhabitants of Broadwindsor hurried to the inn, where they remained locked in loud and acrimonious dispute with the soldiers until, early the next morning, the order was given for the column to fall in and resume its march to the coast. Such a scene is the very stuff of Stuart comedy. One can imagine with what zest Ben Jonson under the first Stuart or Farquhar under the last would have treated it: the bawling, the fist-shaking, the heartless bawdiness of the soldiers teasing the outraged forefathers of the ratepayers association into a frenzy. If no one pitied the mother or was touched by the helplessness of the child, it was an age when life was hard and when there was little to spare.

Charles and his party were no doubt as amused by what they heard as any audience at the Globe or the Haymarket. The affair had robbed them of a night's sleep, but that was a small price to pay for the highly effective distraction of their fellow guests from any unwelcome inquisitiveness about the other inmates of the house. They used their enforced wakefulness to review the situation and discuss plans. Colonel Wyndham was convinced that, though Trent was the safest refuge for the King, it would be most inadvisable to attempt anything further on the Dorset coast, particularly as troops were concentrating on every port to embark for Jersey. He suggested that they should divide forces, the King, Julian Coningsby and himself returning to Trent while Wilmot, guided by Peters, should take up his quarters at the King's Arms in Salisbury, an inn kept by a Royalist of tried loyalty. Peters would there be able to get in touch with a friend and kinsman of Wyndham's, John Coventry, the eldest son by a second marriage of Lord Coventry, Keeper of the Great Seal. Wyndham had already initiated a clandestine correspondence with him in case the Scots invasion should offer a promising opportunity for a Royalist rising. Salisbury would in any case be an excellent centre from which to inquire about the possibilities along the Hampshire and even the Sussex coast. And as it was only thirty miles from Trent communication would be easy and swift. Charles thoroughly approved the scheme. He did not want to make any more forays until a ship had been secured. Wyndham then settled the details of couriers and ciphered messages and thoughtfully arranged that Robert Swan, Lord Wilmot's personal servant, should be sent to join his master at Sherborne the very next day. As soon as the soldiers were well on their way they mounted their horses and Charles and his escort rode quietly back to Trent.

[93]

VIII

Staff Work

WHEN CHARLES looked out of the windows of his handsome panelled rooms in Trent Manor at the familiar view of the church with its spire – a rarity in Somerset and Dorset – across the churchyard where the villagers had so exuberantly celebrated his supposed death, to the landscape of steep green hills rising in soft but brilliant colour above the darker green of ash and chestnut, his relief at finding himself once again in relative safety must have been tinged with frustration. All the excitement of departure, of the secret meeting at the little stone-built thatched farmhouse in the hills above Lyme, of the arrival at the inn within sound of the breakers, of the long night watch when time seemed to stand still, of the hurried flight to Bridport that led into the lion's mouth of danger, of the long ride through the deep overhung lanes to Broadwindsor, had only brought him back to his starting-point. It was now three weeks to the day since the Battle of Worcester, a long time for so conspicuous and well known a figure to have evaded discovery; and here he was, back in this beautiful, secluded village where grey-green and rose lichens patterned the heather-honey colour of the Ham stone of which church and manor and most of the cottages were built. The scene that met his eyes looked tranquillity. But it was not tranquillity he wanted nor, unless he were to betray both himself and his followers, was it attainable.

If at this depressing stage of his adventures Charles had little on which to congratulate himself, the Government had

[94]

less. On September 9th the Council of State discussed the
publication of "penalties against those who harbour Charles
Stuart (or any who have taken arms for him) and for the
encouragement of the discovery of such". The next day they
issued the proclamation, reproduced between pages 112 and 113.
The Press supported these measures with more enthusiasm
than accuracy. *The Faithful Scout* reported in its issue of
September 5th–12th that Charles had been nearly caught by
Colonel Cobbett at Worcester, who had found his George and
Garter.[1] The King had fled towards Wirral and was thought
to be making for the Isle of Man. On September 11th *A
Perfect Diurnall* reported ". . . another party of Scots being
near a thousand were upon Boddeo Downes [Lancashire]
yesterday and asked the way to Stockport, yet we suppose they
will retreat all by way of Carlisle, their King and David Lesley
was with them". On September 13th the *Scout* quoted General
Lambert's opinion that Charles would make for the Highlands
and confidently asserted that "all passes both in England and
Scotland being secured it seems impossible (in humane reason)
that ever the Scots King should escape". But the next day it
printed a letter from Coventry suggesting that Charles was
lurking somewhere in that neighbourhood in company with
Captain Hinde, the highwayman, and darkly supported its
surmise by the fact that some murders had recently been
committed on Meriden Heath. The certitude of the previous
day had been shaken, for the piece concluded: "Some think
him rather to be gone Westward; and yet some imagine he
may as well be about London as anywhere else." The Captain
Hinde theory[2] quickly gained currency. On the following day,
September 15th, a broadside appeared with the title *Another
Victory in Lancashire obtained against the Scots . . . also the Scots*

[1] This was, of course, untrue. See p. 27.

[2] For the curious upshot of this hypothesis and a most interesting account
of Hinde see the essay in C. V. Wedgwood's *Truth and Opinion* (London,
1960).

King going with Hind the great Robber. It could hardly be said to confirm the story, as its only contribution was: "its thought he lies sculking about in some private corners with Hind his guide".

On September 16th the Council of State directed the Committee of Examinations "to use the best means they can for the discovery of Charles Stuart" – a somewhat otiose instruction that perhaps betrays a vague and uncomfortable feeling that someone ought to do something. On the 19th the Militia Commissioners in every county were told to ". . . gather up such prisoners as may yet be lurking in your county; especially let the greatest diligence be used for the discovery and apprehension of Charles Stuart, who was the Commander-in-Chief of that [i.e. the Scots] army, and who we conceive is somewhere hidden in England". That the Council of State had still no particular idea as to where is shewn by an order, dated September 22nd, to Colonel Scroope, the Governor of Bristol. Scroope is warned that the Scots prisoners at Liverpool, Chester, Shrewsbury, Stafford and Worcester are to be brought to Bristol for shipment to the plantations. The absence of any reference to the King in a message dealing with such matters indicates clearly that the authorities had not picked up his trail when he was in those parts barely a week earlier.

On the same day *The Diary* wrote in the sententious tone that, down the ages, bespeaks the strong leader: "There is not a man almost in England but either in his person or discourse is running after the running King of Scotland; some follow him, seeking after publike ends . . . others (of a more sordid temper) . . . would not for a thousand pounds but meet with him. In the meantime it is believed by some that the Scots King hath made a halt in England, and is in a world of perplexities, being not so much afraid of the cloud of bullets that at Worcester came storming in upon him, as of the shower of gold that fell in Danae's lap."

By the end of the week the reading public had two more

accounts to choose from. Under the appropriate heading *Strange News from the King of Scots* some eccentric soldiers from Wakefield published the news that they had heard from William Elliot from Leeds, who was naturally in a position to know, "that the King of Scots is got into Scotland to the Lord Belcarris who with five hundred horse is advanced towards the Marquesse of Argile and the Marquesse of Huntley". As they adorned this information with an allusion to the overthrow of the Athenian tyrant Peisistratus by the Italian historian Guicciardini they had evidently mastered the cardinal principle of journalism that pretentiousness is preferable to accuracy. A day or two later the *Weekly Intelligencer* informed its readers that "It is confirmed by severall personnages of worth that the Earl of Ladderdale [Lauderdale, captured at Worcester and imprisoned in the Tower of London] hath reported that at Worcester fight he saw one of our souldiers make a great blow at the Scots King and that he fell down under the weight and the violence thereof; It is conceived he is dead; and that being stripped of his clothes . . . he was taken the less notice of, his skin being of a sad complexion."

Had Charles been enabled to read all these accounts of his activities his spirits would have risen. But even without this encouragement, the situation very soon began to look more hopeful. The very day of his return to Trent Edward Hyde, Colonel Wyndham's brother-in-law and one of Clarendon's innumerable cousins, came to dinner. During the course of conversation he happened to mention that he had seen Colonel Robert Phelips in Salisbury the day before. Wyndham was quick to perceive the possibilities opened up by this intelligence. Robert Phelips was a younger son of the great family who owned Montacute, still one of the most magnificent houses in the west of England. Their persistent Royalism had led to the sequestration of their estates, which explained Robert Phelips's presence in Salisbury. Besides his undoubted loyalty and valuable connexions Wyndham knew him to be a man of intelligence and resource. He therefore suggested to Charles that Wilmot should be instructed to get in touch with him and, on his ready agreement, got a message away that night by Robert Swan, who was leaving to join his master at Sherborne. With two such useful recruits as John Coventry and Robert Phelips the Wilmot network might achieve something.

Not that Wyndham was content to rely simply on the efforts of his friends in Salisbury. He employed a neighbour, Captain Thomas Littleton, to try the Hampshire coast for a ship. And while all these endeavours were going forward he did not forget his first and quintessential duty of keeping a sharp look-out for any threat to the King's security at Trent. A day or two after the King's return Anne Wyndham made it her business to go into Sherborne "to hear what news there was abroad of the King. And towards evening, at her return, a Troop of horse clapt privately into the town. This silent way of entering their Quarters, in so triumphant a time, gave a strong alarm to this careful lady, whose thoughts were much troubled concerning her Royal Guest. A stop she made to hearken out what brought them thither, and whither they were bound: but not one grain of Intelligence could be procured by the most industrious enquiry." She hurried home, where Charles, seeing that she was worried, inquired the cause. When she told him "his Majesty laughed most heartily, as if he had not been in the least concerned". The Colonel, however, agreed with his wife in taking a serious view of this development, and persuaded the King to enter the secret chamber concealed behind the panelling. Charles soon re-emerged but promised to retreat there at the least approach of danger. All that night the Colonel kept strict watch. He was the more anxious because he had received news from Sherborne that the troop did not intend to quarter there but only to halt for refreshment. This intelligence proved accurate. About two in the morning they resumed their march, which, to everyone's

[98]

relief, lay towards the coast. Like the soldiers at Bridport and Broadwindsor, they were evidently bound for Jersey.

Meanwhile, Wilmot had been getting on famously. He arrived at the King's Arms in Salisbury on September 25th and at once established contact with Coventry and Phelips. Coventry came to see him first and was in full possession of the facts by the time Phelips joined them. Phelips had, one need hardly say, served under Wilmot during the war, but unlike most others who had had this privilege he had his doubts as to whether his old Commander-in-Chief was quite the man to go tiger-shooting with. As a west-countryman he would certainly recollect Wilmot's distinctly equivocal relations with Essex, the Parliamentary General, which caused Charles I to deprive him of his command in the west in the summer of 1644. And he says himself that he treated Wilmot coldly because he understood that "he had too warmly engaged with Argyle's faction in Scotland". Indeed, on any objective view a true-blue Royalist had every reason to be wary of him. John Coventry evidently thought the Colonel a little reserved, so he excused himself to smoke a pipe of tobacco with the landlord.

As soon as they were by themselves Wilmot overcame the Colonel's caution by telling him that the King was in hiding at Trent and had commissioned him to say that he knew not how to dispose of himself and that he would commit himself to Colonel Phelips to provide for his security. To a man of his principles there could be but one answer to such an appeal, but he gave it with the fullest acknowledgment both of the difficulties of the undertaking and of his own readiness to pledge his own life as a surety for the King's. At this point Coventry rejoined them. " 'Well, gentlemen, are you agreed?' 'Twas answered 'yes' ", so Wilmot, relapsing thankfully into the familiar joys of the Officers' Mess, called for "a bottle or two" and regaled them both with an account of the King's adventures since the Battle of Worcester. No doubt the acute Colonel Phelips drew his own conclusions as to Wilmot's discretion.

After they parted for the night Wilmot sent Henry Peters back to Trent "with this joyful message . . . that he doubted not . . . to be able in some short time to effect his desires". Phelips would probably have thought this premature: but then he was the man who would actually have to do the work.

He lost no time in setting about it. Early the next morning he went to Southampton to see a merchant named Horne with whom he was on very good terms. Horne was away from home but was expected back the next day, so Colonel Phelips left a letter for him saying that he wished to see him on particularly urgent business and, as he would be staying at Colonel St. Barbe's house only six miles out of Southampton, he would be grateful if Horne would come and see him there next day if he got home in time. Horne returned home early the next morning and came straight out to Colonel St. Barbe's where he found the household at dinner. They finished the meal and then Phelips and Horne took a stroll in the garden. Phelips told the merchant that he needed a ship to carry himself and a friend or two over to France. After a moment's reflection Horne answered, " 'There is such a man, who is now at home and his bark, so honest a fellow that I would trust ten thousand lives, if I were master of as many, in his hands; and I will make haste home and speak with him.' Then said the Colonel: 'Do not only speak with him but come to some agreement with him.' " This Horne agreed to do and, prudently anxious that Phelips should not be seen in Southampton again, promised to bring the man out to meet him at Redbridge at three o'clock the next afternoon, which was a Sunday. He was as good as his word and terms were quickly agreed. The master was to receive a total payment of £40, of which he required an immediate advance of £20 as his ship was laid up and he needed the money to sign on a crew and provision her. For his part he undertook that the vessel should be riding at anchor between Southampton and Calshot Castle by the following Wednesday, October 1st, on which day the Colonel was to return to see that all was ready. Phelips at once returned to Salisbury to tell Wilmot of his success and sent his brother, Colonel Edward Phelips, over to Trent to deliver the good news to the King. On the same day, September 28th, Captain Thomas Littleton reported to Colonel Wyndham from Hampshire that he had been in negotiation with the master of a ship "who undertook to carry off the Lord Wilmot and his company, upon the condition his lordship would follow his direction" – a proviso that suggests that this unknown mariner was either possessed of unusual foresight or had been one of Wilmot's many comrades-in-arms. Presented with this choice Wyndham unhesitatingly decided to rely on Phelips and ordered Littleton to return to Trent and not to proceed with his arrangements until further orders.

As the enterprise was developing so fast and favourably Phelips and Coventry were anxious that Charles should shift his quarters nearer to the scene of action. They fixed on Heale House, some three miles out of Salisbury, standing in a secluded position on the banks of the Avon, as the most suitable place. Certainly its owner, Mrs. Amphillis Hyde, widow of one of Clarendon's first cousins, was, as Phelips described her, "a worthy discreet loyall lady". Accordingly Coventry's domestic chaplain was dispatched to Trent with a letter containing this proposal "rolled up into a bigness of a musket bullet, which the faithful messenger had order to swallow down his throat in case of any danger". Charles did not accept with the alacrity that might have been expected. Time must have been hanging heavy at Trent, since, as before, he was reduced to boring holes through gold coins and cooking his own meals, diversions which suggest the extremities of tedium. Perhaps he was understandably reluctant to move back into Wilmot's orbit until the situation absolutely demanded it; perhaps, too, he over-estimated the security of Trent. The villagers, we know, were hot Cromwellians and their curiosity might be stimulated by the arrival and departure of unfamiliar couriers such as Edward Phelips and John Coventry's chaplain. He wrote back "that he desired all diligence might be used in providing a vessel, and if it should prove difficult at [South]Hampton, trial should be made farther; that they should be ascertained of a ship before they sent to remove him, that so he might run no more hazards than what of necessity he must meet with in his passage from Trent to the place of his transportation".

This was on October 1st, the day on which Colonel Phelips was to meet the master of the ship and confirm that all was ready. To his great disappointment he found that the ship had been pressed to carry provisions to the fleet that was lying off Jersey under Blake. With characteristic energy and strength of mind he determined to abandon Southampton altogether and to try an entirely new field. Returning to Salisbury he consulted Coventry and their common friend Dr. Humphrey Henchman (as they had better things to do than reminisce over the bottle, Wilmot was not invited to join them). Henchman had, in fact, been in their counsels from the beginning and had suggested Heale House as a convenient base for the King. As the only clergyman of the Church of England to play an important part in the King's escape he deserves a little introduction. Born under Queen Elizabeth, he spent the greater part of James I's reign at Cambridge, where he became a Fellow of Clare Hall and laid the foundations of his wide scholarship. He spent the twenty years before the Civil War as Precentor and Canon of Salisbury from which, as from his other preferments, he was ejected by the victorious Parliament. He continued to live in the Close and was made Bishop of Salisbury by Charles II on his Restoration in 1660. Three years later he became Bishop of London and held the see till his death in 1675. Like the King, he set an example of calm courage by remaining at his post throughout the great plague of 1665 during which, deserted by his officials, he took the lead in organising measures of relief. After the Great Fire in the following year he devoted most of his energy and much of his own money to the rebuilding of St. Paul's and of the Bishop's Palace in Aldersgate Street, soon to be forsaken by his successors for the more agreeable country retreat of Fulham. Although a firm and uncompromising High Churchman his episcopate was characterised by a marked refusal to persecute or interfere with dissenters. Baxter, a divine of very different opinions whose vivid recollection of the routed Royalists passing through Kidderminster has been quoted earlier, came up against him at the Savoy Conference of 1661 and was impressed as much by his dignity and gentleness as by his great learning.[1] Nothing of a politician, still less of a toady, Henchman exemplifies the peculiar excellences of the Laudian churchmen without that rough, bullying streak that disfigures so many of them. The portrait by Lely (reproduced facing p. 112) shows a face kindly, serious, sensitive and magnanimous. But perhaps the most eloquent tribute to him is the fact that men of such discernment as Phelips and Coventry should have wanted to take an old clergyman of sixty (and one was old at sixty in the seventeenth century) into their entire confidence in so important and dangerous a matter.

At this conference it was agreed that the Sussex coast would be the best place to try. There at least their plans should be safe from dislocation by the incessant demands of the expedition against Jersey. Colonel Phelips then suggested that they should approach his friend Colonel George Gunter of Racton, near Chichester. This was warmly approved by Henchman, who also knew him well. Phelips therefore wrote a letter to Gunter to be delivered by Mrs. Gunter's nephew, Lawrence Hyde[2] of Hinton Daubnay in Hampshire. Finally they resolved that in spite of the reluctant tone of Charles's latest message

[1] "Insight" is the word he uses: the highest praise one scholar can bestow on another.

[2] Gunter had married Katharine Hyde, first cousin to Clarendon and sister-in-law to Mrs. Hyde of Heale House.

no time must be lost in removing him from Trent to Heale House. Once these decisions had been reached it was clearly impracticable not to inform Wilmot. Perhaps tact made it necessary to suppress the fact of the Phelips–Coventry–Henchman conference and to represent its conclusions as suggestions tentatively offered for his approval. Perhaps Phelips was blunter and affronted Wilmot's self-importance. We have no account of the meeting, but we do know that Phelips's letter to Gunter was never delivered as Wilmot, perhaps feeling himself cut off from the centre of action in his snug quarters at the King's Arms, decided to handle the matter in person. What alarm this caused to his fellow conspirators one can only guess. But off he set, complete with Robert Swan, to call on Lawrence Hyde at Hinton Daubnay. As a gesture in the direction of disguise he hit upon the idea of calling himself Mr. Barlow, but this does not seem to have prevented startled recognition from all those he visited. In addition to Lawrence Hyde he called, apparently on his own initiative, on a Mr. Thomas Henslow at Burchant, near Titchfield, the house of the Earl of Southampton, one of Charles I's great officers of state and one of the four bearers at his funeral. Henslow passed on Wilmot's news to Lord Southampton, who at once offered the King his personal protection and undertook to find him a ship. Although events made it unnecessary to take advantage of this it is remarkable as being the only contribution to the King's escape made by a Royalist of the front rank; sufficiently remarkable for Charles to remember the old man's courage and generosity when he came to dictate his account to Pepys thirty years later.

On his arrival at Hinton Daubnay, Wilmot, with his usual luck, found that Captain Thomas Gunter, a cousin of Colonel George Gunter, was actually staying in the house. His onward journey to Racton was thus easily arranged.

While Wilmot was engaged in Hampshire and Sussex, Phelips had set out for Trent to overcome the King's reluctance to move on to Heale and to conduct him there in person. He arrived at Trent on Sunday, October 5th, and the King, swayed by the unanimity of Phelips, Coventry and Wilmot, capitulated and agreed to leave the next day. As before he was to assume the character of a mounted servant and Julian Coningsby was to ride pillion. They were to be accompanied as far as Heale by the invaluable Henry Peters, but not, in spite of repeated petitions to be allowed to attend him to the point of embarkation, by Colonel Wyndham. As Charles pointed out, "it was no way necessary, and might prove very inconvenient. But [he] sweetened his denial with this promise, that if he were put to any distress, he would again retreat to Trent.

"About ten the next morning, October the sixth, his majesty took leave of the old Lady Wyndham, the colonel's lady [Anne Wyndham, from whom this passage is quoted] and family, not omitting the meanest of them that served him; but to the good old lady he vouchsafed more than ordinary respect, who accounted it her highest honour that she had had three sons and one grandchild slain in the defence of the father, and that she herself, in her old age, had been instrumental in the protection of the son, both kings of England.

"Thus his sacred majesty . . . bad farewel to Trent, the ark in which God shut him up when the floods of rebellion had covered the face of his dominions."

He had spent, altogether, nineteen days there.

IX

Colonel Gunter

COLONEL GEORGE GUNTER of Racton belongs, like his friends Henchman and Phelips, to that section of the Royalist party, serious, educated, devout, its mainstay in the storm of war, whose natural leaders were Falkland, Clarendon and Ormonde, men whom Charles I did not favour until he was forced to nor Charles II retain when he felt free to let them go. Nearly of an age with Henchman, he shared with Phelips the common background of a country gentleman who had been educated at Oxford. Although he was in his fiftieth year when the Civil War broke out he served as a regimental officer. The formidable expense of his service (a Royalist officer was not paid, but rather required to pay for the maintenance of the men and horses he brought with him) bore crushingly on a small estate; and his stout refusal to recognise the legitimacy of the Commonwealth Government involved him in further heavy payments to the Committee for Compounding. By the autumn of 1651 he was, financially, in very low water; and his uncompromising Royalism kept him confined to a five mile radius of his house. It speaks volumes for a man so situated that his friends should have thought of him as the person to smuggle the King out of the country.

But by what Gunter himself evidently considered a miraculous intervention his increasing misfortune was made the instrument of a fortune beyond his dreams. "In the very nick of time when he was first thought upon for so great a work comes a messenger with a warrant from the Commissioners of

[106]

Haberdasher's Hall, London, to summon him to appear before them within ten days to pay two hundred pounds for his five-and-twentieth part;[1] which they had set upon him upon pain of sequestration on default.

"He first refused, and told the messenger he was confined and would not go five miles from home; but he left with him the order and told him it should be at his peril if he did not obey it.

"The colonel the next day repaired to Chichester, four miles from him, to the Commissioners there, to show them his order. They peremptorily replied he must go and his order would bear him out. He went accordingly and compounded with them and got off £100 of the two hundred he was set at; but his credit being shaken, the current running then so hard against the King, the royal party, and all good men, that he could not borrow the money in all London, he was forced with all speed to repair into the country, and went privately to his usurer, who had the security of his whole estate.

"He shewed him his danger and requested to borrow one hundred pounds, upon his bond and his former security; who readily condescended, and told him out the money. The next day he was to call for it and seal the bond. He had no sooner ended this business, being stayed somewhat longer by some friends then he intended, but that very night he came home (being 7th Oct. 1651) he found some at his house who were come about this design.

"I think it will easily be granted by any that reads and considers, that this was not without a providence, since that it is apparent that if his friends had come before he had been licensed to go abroad, he must needs have been excused; and if they had come much after, it was possible a new restraint might have come between, or his liberty in going so freely up and down after his business ended, most suspected."

[1] i.e. one twenty-fifth of the value at which the Committee for Compounding had assessed his estate.

When Colonel Gunter returned home between eight and nine o'clock that evening his wife met him at the door and told him that there was a Devonshire gentleman in the parlour, sent by Lawrence Hyde, "about a reference which none beside yourself can decide". On entering the room he found the Devonshire gentleman sitting on one side of the fire and his cousin Captain Thomas Gunter at the other. A few years later, shortly before his death, he recollected the scene with extreme distinctness:

"The gentleman rose and saluted him. The colonel presently[1] knew him to be the Lord Wilmot, which the noble lord perceiving took the colonel aside to the window; 'I see you know me' (said he), 'do not own me.' Captain Thomas Gounter, the colonel's kinsman for all he had a long time been in the army and under his command, knew him not, which was strange, the noble lord being but meanly disguised. After a bottle of sack, which afforded some matter of discourse, by reason of two wasps or rather hornets which came out at the opening, a short collation being made ready as soon as could (his lady having given leave to her servants to be from home that day), my lord's man, one Swan, coming in to wait, whispered his master in the ear, and told him my Lord Wentworth's boy Lonie was without; and wished him to be careful for fear the boy should know him, being taken by Captain Thomas Gounter in distress at Chelsea, and clothed by him to wait upon him."

This was not the only occasion on which Swan's alertness prevented the worst consequences of his master's irresponsible behaviour. Lord Wentworth's boy Lonie would certainly have recognised him (Captain Thomas Gunter is the only recorded case of anyone's failure to do so) as his old employer was a particular friend of Wilmot's and had even protested against his dismissal in 1644. None of this was lost upon Mrs. Gunter. When they were clearing away the cold supper she confided in

[1] At once.

her husband's cousin that she was sure that Mr. Barlow, the Devonshire gentleman, was really someone else in disguise.

Soon after supper "the colonel offered the noble lord, then by name Mr. Barlowe, it being late and as the greatest courtesy he could then show him, to wait upon him to his chamber, and to bed which he readily accepted.

"The colonel took up the candle, the noble lord following him, his lady and kinsman attending.

"When he came into the chamber, it being late the colonel desired his lady and kinsman to go to bed and to leave him for he was bound to wait upon this gentleman awhile, they took leave and bid him goodnight.

"The noble lord and colonel being alone, he broke the business unto the colonel with these words (sighing): 'The King of England, my master, your master and the master of all good Englishmen, is near you and in great distress; can you help us to a boat?'. The colonel looking very sadly, after some pause, said, 'Is he well? Is he safe?' He said 'Yes'. The colonel replied 'God be blessed', and gave him a reason for his question if he should not be secure, he doubted not but he could secure him till a boat could be gotten."

Wilmot, of course, had left Salisbury before the outcome of Phelips's mission to Trent could be known. In fact the King had arrived safely at Heale House the previous evening, but it was a day or two before he and Gunter learned of this. He said that he hoped the King was out of danger at present and that he intended to bring him to stay at Racton in a short time. "The colonel's thoughts were much raised in expectation of such a guest", but, sensible, practical man that he was, he at once recognised the advantages of Heale on hearing of the arrangement. They then passed to the crucial business of getting a ship. "The colonel told the lord seriously, and nothing but the truth, that for all he lived so near the sea, yet there was no man living so little acquainted with these kind of men." However he hastened to add that that would not prevent him from doing his utmost to preserve his King. "The noble lord . . . was abundantly satisfied with this answer, hugging him in his arms and kissed his cheek again and again." The Colonel then said goodnight and told him to sleep well as he would keep watch "and that he doubted not but in good time all would be well".

Leaving Wilmot with this comforting assurance the Colonel retired to his own room. What followed deserves to be quoted in his own words, as much for the glimpse of a perfect marriage as for their eloquent authenticity.

"Coming into his chamber, he found his wife had stayed up for him, and was very earnest to know who this was, and what was his business. The colonel desired her to excuse him, assuring her it was nothing concerning her, or that would anyways damnify her.

"She was confident there was more in it than so, and enough she doubted to ruin him and all his family;[1] and in that, said she, I am concerned, breaking out into a very great passion of weeping. Which the colonel seeing took a candle, pretending to go into the next room, but privately to my Lord Wilmot, and acquainted him how it was, asking his advice, whether as the case stood it were any way amiss to acquaint her with it; that he durst pass his word for the loyalty and integrity of his wife; however, without his allowance, she should know nothing.

"The noble lord replied: 'No, no; by all means acquaint her with it.'

"He humbly thanked him and bade him goodnight again. The colonel coming into his chamber unfolded the business, wiped the tears off his lady's eyes, who smiling, said: 'Go on and prosper; yet I fear you will hardly do it.'

" 'However,' said the colonel, 'I must endeavour, and will do my best, leaving the success to God Almightly.' His lady deporting herself during the whole carriage of the business,

[1] Apart from a number of elder children Mrs. Gunter had two little boys of six and four and a baby born in the spring of that year.

with so much discretion, courage, and fidelity, that (without vanity be it spoken) she seemed, her danger considered, to outgo her sex. Neither will the reader think this an impertinent circumstance, since the success of the business did not a little depend on her concurrence.''

The Colonel, as he tells us, contented himself with very little sleep that night. Early the next morning, Wednesday, October 8th, he rode over to Emsworth, then a favourite harbour for fishing smacks and coasters, taking with him an old servant who was related to some of the seamen who were known to use the port. On that day, however, none of them were about, so Gunter turned for home to report to Wilmot, who had promised not to stir outside until he got back. But Wilmot was not the man to be restrained by promises from his itch to meddle in anything which gave the appearance of action. Half a mile from Racton Gunter met him on horseback, accompanied by Robert Swan. He told him that he had drawn blank at Emsworth (where, four years later, at the conclusion of Wilmot's second foray into England, Gunter was to find him a ship) and suggested that they should try Langstone Harbour. As they were riding along Wilmot put his hand in his pocket and discovered that he had left all his money behind. Impatient to be up and doing, he must have left it in his bed at Racton. The invaluable Swan was dispatched to retrieve it and found that Mrs. Gunter, startled and surprised to hear that Wilmot had left the house, had been into his room and found a black purse full of gold lying in the middle of his bed. This, of course, was the money provided by Giles Strangways of Melbury Court to serve as the King's emergency ration of cash. Even at this distance of time one can feel an aghast echo of what those who were risking not only their own lives but the safety of their wives and children must have felt at Wilmot's slackness and unreliability. Yet many of them, among them Colonel Gunter, seem to have felt an indulgent, amused but none the less real affection for him, in spite of his awe-inspiring incompetence. The convivial military buffoon, from Falstaff to Captain Grimes or Colonel Chinstrap, is a perennially endearing figure.

At Langstone they had no better luck than at Emsworth – except that Wilmot and Gunter had oysters for luncheon. Wilmot and Swan then mounted their horses and departed for Lawrence Hyde's house at Hinton Daubnay, which was to be their advanced base. The Colonel returned to Racton where, taking his cousin Thomas into the secret, he sent him off to try various other places and arranged to meet him in Chichester the next day. He then rode back to Hinton Daubnay to give Wilmot an account of these measures. After supper, "it being a very dismal night for wind and rain", Wilmot pressed him to stay, but the Colonel refused, "replying that delays were dangerous, and let the weather be what it would, he had a sure guide". He reached home between one and two in the morning, lay down on his bed for a couple of hours, and then set out for Chichester to keep his appointment with his cousin. Thomas Gunter had recruited yet another kinsman, and between them they had quartered the inlets of Chichester Harbour without success.

Reflecting on this discouraging situation, the Colonel decided to approach a merchant in the French trade, a certain Francis Mansell, who lived in Chichester. It was a bold move as Gunter only knew him by sight, having met him casually in the company of other people. He went to call on him "pretending to give him a visit and to be better acquainted with him. He received him courteously and entertained him with a bottle or two of his French wine and Spanish tobacco. After a while the colonel broke the business to him, saying: 'I do not only come to visit you, but I must request one favour of you.' He replied: Anything in his power. Then the colonel asked him if he could freight a bark, for, said he, 'I have two special friends of mine who have been engaged in a duel, and there is mischief done, and I am obliged to get them off if I can.' "

Dr. Humphrey Henchman

Sir Peter Lely

The *Royal Escape,* formerly the coal-brig *Surprise*

Van de Velde

21

By the Parliament.

A PROCLAMATION
FOR THE
Diſcovery and Apprehending of *CHARLS STVART*, and other Traytors
his Adherents and Abettors.

Whereas CHARLS STUART Son to the late Tyrant, with divers of the Engliſh and Scotiſh Nation, have lately in a Trayterous and Hoſtile maner with an Army invaded this Nation, which by the Bleſſing of God upon the Forces of this Commonwealth have been defeated, and many of the chief Actors therein ſlain and taken priſoners; but the ſaid Charls Stuart is eſcaped: For the ſpeedy Apprehending of ſuch a Malicious and Dangerous Traytor to the Peace of this Commonwealth, The Parliament doth ſtraightly Charge and Command all Officers, as well Civil as Military, and all other the good People of this Nation, That they make diligent Search and Enquiry for the ſaid Charls Stuart, and his Abettors and Adherents in this Invaſion, and uſe their beſt Endeavors for the Diſcovery and Arreſting the Bodies of them and every of them; and being apprehended, to bring or cauſe to be brought forthwith and without delay, in ſafe Cuſtody before the Parliament or Council of State, to be proceeded with and ordered as Juſtice ſhall require; And if any perſon ſhall knowingly Conceal the ſaid Charls Stuart, or any his Abettors or Adherents, or ſhall not Reveal the Places of their Abode or Being, if it be in their power ſo to do, The Parliament doth Declare, That they will hold them as partakers and Abettors of their Trayterous and Wicked Practices and Deſigns: And the Parliament doth further Publiſh and Declare, That whoſoever ſhall apprehend the perſon of the ſaid Charls Stuart, and ſhall bring or cauſe him to be brought to the Parliament or Council of State, ſhall have given and beſtowed on him or them as a Reward for ſuch Service, the ſum of One thouſand pounds; And all Officers, Civil and Military, are required to be aiding and aſſiſting unto ſuch perſon and perſons therein. Given at Weſtminſter this Tenth day of September, One thouſand ſix hundred fifty one.

Wedneſday the Tenth of September. 1651.

ORdered by the Parliament, That this Proclamation be forthwith Printed and Publiſhed.

Hen: Scobell, Cleric. Parliamenti.

London, Printed by *John Field*, Printer to the Parliament of *England*. 1651.

The proclamation of the reward for the King's capture, September 10, 1651

Colonel Gunter in 1642

The King and Carlis in the oak tree.

In this series of paintings by Isaac Fuller recording the early stages of the escape (now in the Banqueting House at Whitehall) the romantic and decorative potentialities of the subject take precedence over fidelity to detail.

Isaac Fuller's view of the night ride from Boscobel to Moseley

Mansell thought he knew of a possibility at Brighton. Gunter pressed him to go with him then and there and offered him £50 if he could settle the matter immediately. But it happened to be the day of one of the most important fairs at Chichester and Mansell's partner was away from home. He agreed, however, to go with him the next day, Friday the 10th.

Colonel Gunter had undertaken to report progress to Wilmot once every twelve hours or, at the very outside, every twenty-four. He was thus faced with another long ride of twenty miles or so to Hinton Daubnay, which he could not reach until evening, followed by another night ride back to Chichester so as to be ready to escort Mansell to Brighton in the morning. After two nights virtually without sleep it was a prospect that might have daunted a far younger man. As he would need his wits about him on the morrow he would have been amply justified in sending his cousin Thomas in his place. But Colonel Gunter's standards, like his stamina, were not those of an ordinary man. He reported in person to Wilmot, "who approved and liked the way wondrous well". It was, he tells us, very late and "very dark and boisterous weather" when he took his leave. "His horse being almost spent, he borrowed a horse of his kinsman, Mr. Hyde, who lent him his falconer's horse, being, as it seems, the best he then had, which served to carry him home, and the next morning to Chichester."

Once again the only rest he got was a cat-nap at Racton in the small hours. Mansell was punctual to his appointment but had no horse, so Gunter lent him the falconer's animal and borrowed one for himself from his cousin Thomas. He instructed Thomas to report his departure from Chichester in Mansell's company to Wilmot and to remain at Hinton Daubnay at his disposal until further orders.

He and Mansell then set out for Brighton, where they arrived at two o'clock in the afternoon. Mansell at once inquired for the man he had in mind, only to be told that he had sailed for

Chichester, where he was in negotiation for a freight. What Gunter must have felt after all those hours in the saddle can only be imagined as, characteristically, he records the fact without comment. But, unexpectedly, their luck was in. News came that he had put in at Shoreham, only four miles away. Gunter insisted that Mansell should send to him immediately to come and see him on urgent business. This took effect and early that evening their visitor was announced.

Nicholas Tettersell, master and owner of the coal-brig *Surprise* (thirty-four tons), was a native of Brighton and an experienced Channel seaman. He belongs to a type, now all but extinct since the decay in the last fifty years of the inshore fishery and the coastal trade, which altered perhaps less than any other in our society between the Norman conquest, and the death of Queen Victoria. One says "in our society", but really one means on the fringes of it, not only because of the obvious fact of geography but by the nature of the life they led, isolated from the world behind the harbour and untouched by social and technological change. Colonel Gunter had recognised this when he told Wilmot that though he had lived all his life next door to these people he knew absolutely nothing about them. Being the sensible man that he was he had stipulated that Mansell should conduct the negotiation, "being his affair and trade, he to sit by as neuter, promising the merchant to make good and to pay him whatever he should agree for, but withal desired to get it as low as he could".

It was not an easy affair. Tettersell stayed with them overnight and it was not until two o'clock on the Saturday afternoon that a satisfactory agreement was reached. Tettersell, not unreasonably, refused to discuss terms until he had been told whom or what he was to carry, so Mansell, who had not been admitted to the secret, was forced to tell him, in good faith, Gunter's cover story about the two duellists who found it necessary to put themselves out of reach of the law. Satisfied with this explanation, Tettersell demanded a down-payment of

£60 and promised for his part to have his ship at an hour's notice for sea. As Gunter now had to arrange for the King's journey to Brighton and could not say for certain when he would arrive, he persuaded Mansell to stay on at Brighton "under pretence of freighting his bark" to see that everything was ready. In addition to his expenses he promised Mansell £50 for his trouble.

Having settled all this Gunter mounted his horse about three o'clock and rode off to report to Wilmot. He arrived at Hinton Daubnay, after a ride of forty-odd miles, between eight and nine that night, only to find that Wilmot was spending the night at the house of a tenant of Lawrence Hyde's who was married to Thomas Gunter's sister. But this was more than offset by the unexpected presence of Robin Phelips, who had come to Hinton Daubnay to find out how Gunter was getting on and was at that moment just about to go to bed. He and Lawrence Hyde were burning to know the latest developments, and when Gunter told them "that all things were well and in readiness, the noble Colonel Phelips replied, 'Thou shalt be a saint in my almanack for ever' ". It was a fitting recognition of his prodigious exertions.

How much these had told on his constitution his friends easily saw. Lawrence Hyde urged him to get a night's sleep and go over and tell Wilmot in the morning, but he considered himself bound in honour to give his account without delay. At this Phelips insisted on going with him: anyway, by the standards of his recent journeys, it was not very far. Wilmot "was infinitely pleased and satisfied" when he heard his full report and at once opened the question of who should go for the King. "It was agreed that Colonel Phelips should, by reason that Colonel Gounter was much tired out, and would need rest for further employment." So early the next morning, Sunday, October 12th, Colonel Phelips set out for Heale while his old friend enjoyed the deep, satisfying sleep that follows physical exhaustion and duty done.

X

A Trip to Brighton

T HE KING, it will be remembered, had left Trent on Monday, October 6th, accompanied by Henry Peters, Julian Coningsby and Colonel Phelips. It was not a difficult journey, by way of Wincanton and Mere, and Phelips tells us that he "knowing all that country perfectly well brought them in such private ways that they came near very few houses, only the King being hungry would needs go into Mere (which could have been left on the left hand) and there at a true loyal Innkeepers they dined". A fuller description of the meal is given in one of the earliest and best accounts[1] of the King's adventures to be published after the Restoration:

"The host sate at the table with His Majesty, and administered matters of discourse, told the Colonel for news that he heard the men of Westminster (meaning the rebels) notwithstanding their victory at Worcester were in a great maze, not knowing what was become of the King; but (says he) 'tis the most received opinion that he is come in a disguise to London, and many houses have been searched for him there, at which His Majesty was observed to smile.

"After dinner mine host familiarly asked the King if he were a friend to Caesar to which His Majesty answered Yes, then said he, here's a health to King Charles, in a glass of wine, His Majesty and the Colonel both pledged."

Charles himself has described their arrival at Heale, which they reached without further incident:

[1] Blount's *Boscobel*. This and other sources are discussed on pp. 149–154.

"I came into the house, just as it was almost dark, with Robin Philips only, not intending at first to make myself known. But just as I alighted at the door Mrs. Hyde knew me, though she had never seen me but once in her life, and that was with the King, my father, in the army, when we marched by Salisbury, some years before, in the time of war; but she being a discreet woman took no notice at that time of me, I passing only for a friend of Robin Philips', by whose advice I went thither.

"At supper there was with us Frederick Hyde, since a judge, and his sister-in-law, a widow,[1] Robin Philips, myself and Dr. Henshaw,[2] since Bishop of London, whom I had appointed to meet me there.

"While we were at supper I observed Mrs. Hyde and her brother Frederick to look a little earnestly at me, which led me to believe they might know me. But I was not at all startled at it, it having been my purpose to let her know who I was; and accordingly after supper Mrs. Hyde came to me, and I discovered myself to her; who told me she had a very safe place to hide me in, till we knew whether our ship was ready or no. But she said it was not safe for her to trust any body but herself and her sister; and therefore advised me to take my horse next morning, and make as if I quitted the house, and return again about night; for she would order it so that all her servants and everybody should be out of the house, but herself and her sister, whose name I remember not."

The reason why Frederick Hyde, who was ignorant of the identity of his fellow guest, stared at him at dinner was, surely, that his clothes and general appearance did not fit either the way in which he was treated in the house or the tone

---

[1] i.e. his hostess, Mrs. Hyde.

[2] The King's memory for the names of persons and places was understandably sketchy after such a lapse of time. But it does seem extraordinary that he should not recall Henchman's name, as he had died only five years earlier.

and matter of his conversation. Charles was playing the part of Robin Phelips's friend, which meant, more or less, being himself, but he was still wearing the suit of coarse grey cloth that belonged to the role of Will Jackson, the tenant's son. Mrs. Hyde, we are told, ". . . though His Majesty was set at the lower end of the table, yet the good gentlewoman had much ado to overcome herself, and not come to him first, however she could not refrain from drinking to him in a glass of wine, and giving him two larks where others had but one." No wonder the observant lawyer concluded that there was more than met the eye. This impression was strengthened when talking to him after supper he ". . . wondered to receive such rational discourse from a person whose habit spoke him but of mean degree". The discrepancy arose from the fact that Will Jackson was an admirable part in which to make the journey from Trent as Julian Coningsby's attendant but raised altogether too many complications to be worth establishing at Heale. Julian herself would have had to stay in the house for a start, and, as she had already served her purpose by his arrival there, that would have been, in Charles's own expression to Colonel Wyndham, "in no way necessary and might prove very inconvenient". We do not, in fact, know when he parted from her or where she spent the night. We know from Charles's own account already quoted that he arrived at Heale "with Robin Phelips only" and we know from Phelips that Julian, accompanied by Henry Peters, returned to Trent the next day.

When the King went up to bed Henchman came with him and had a long talk. Among other things it was settled that he should act as post-office for the letters from Wilmot and Phelips and should pass them on to the King through Mrs. Hyde. The next morning, in accordance with her instructions, Charles and Phelips left Heale and "rid about the downs and viewed Stonehenge and found that the King's Arithmetick gave the lie to that fabulous tale that those stones cannot be told[1] alike twice together. This was rather necessity than curiosity for that day being a fair day at Salisbury Mrs. Hyde gave leave to all the servants to go thither whilst the King who went away in their sight with Colonel Phelips in the morning, returned to Heale again in their absence''. They were met by Henchman and Mrs. Hyde, who took the King through the silent house to a secret chamber where he was to remain until he heard that a ship was ready for him. It sounds rather depressing, but all Charles says about it is that it was ''very convenient and safe''; he was visited only by Mrs. Hyde and her sister, who brought him his meals and the letters that Henchman received from Wilmot and Phelips.

Phelips left Heale that same afternoon, leading the King's horse to the house of a friend a few miles away to be stabled there. He then set off to find out how Gunter was getting on and what Wilmot was up to. Both questions were answered, as we know, late on the night of Saturday, October 11th. Sunday morning saw him hurrying back to Salisbury with his joyful news. He settled the details of the King's departure with Henchman, who went out to Heale that evening to tell him of Gunter's success and to prepare for the journey. Phelips was to appear ''at the meadow gate opening into the river'' between two and three in the morning, leading the King's horse. He arrived in good time, but while he was waiting the led horse broke his bridle and galloped off up the river. Catching a runaway horse in broad daylight in enclosed country is not always easy. In the middle of the night with the confounded animal curvetting gaily up the banks of a river, liable, at every step, to break its leg in a trailing rein, it must have been anxious work, but Colonel Phelips was equal to it. Even when he had caught the horse he was still faced with the problem of the broken bridle. The mending of it was, he tells us, ''no small trouble, but at length, with a strong ribbon which Mrs. Hyde helped them to, things were in a tolerable

[1] Counted.

[119]

manner amended''. She and Henchman must have seen them off with relief.

Leaving Salisbury well to the south, they headed east-south-east across a stretch of country even today well-wooded and thinly populated. They were making for Warnford Downs, a few miles west of Petersfield, where Wilmot and Gunter were to meet them. Colonel Gunter, much refreshed by thirty-six hours off duty, suggested to Wilmot and his cousin Thomas over dinner at Hinton Daubnay that they should borrow a brace of greyhounds so that they could make a pretence of coursing on the downs that afternoon. The proposal was approved and he rode over to his married sister's house at the next village of Hambledon to get them, telling her that ''. . . his cousin Gounter and other gentlemen were upon the downs and had a mind to have a course at a hare; and it was possible, if they did not beat too far, and should stay out late, they might all come and be merry with her that night – however, she should be sure of her dogs. 'If you do you shall be heartily welcome' was her answer.''

After a while the Colonel grew impatient with the sport and, leaving the other two (or rather three, for Robert Swan was, of course, in attendance on his Lordship), he decided to ride on by himself and meet the King. Just as he was coming into the village of Warnford he saw Phelips and the King riding towards him. As he was so close to the houses he thought it might draw attention if he were to turn his horse and ride back on his tracks with them, so he passed them without any sign of recognition and went to an inn where he ''called for some beer and took a pipe, and stayed so long that they were atop Old Winchester[1] before he overtook them''. Of all the Royalist gentry who assisted the King Colonel Gunter showed the highest natural aptitude for underground work.

[1] Old Winchester Hill stands about two miles to the south-east of Warnford.

When he caught up with them, he paid his respects to the King and showed them which direction they should take. He then rode on ahead to find Wilmot and the others and brought them all together. Wilmot and the King had a private conversation and then, as they came to Broadhalfpenny Down, the King asked Gunter where he could find a lodging in the neighbourhood. Gunter replied that he was expected at Lawrence Hyde's house at Hinton Daubnay, two miles further on, and Wilmot mentioned the house of Lord Southampton's neighbour, which would have meant a detour of ten or fifteen miles to the south-west. Charles, who had ridden forty miles already, saw no reason to extend his journey unnecessarily. But to Gunter's puzzlement he was evidently reluctant to stay at Hyde's house.[1] " 'Know you no other?' he said. 'Yes, may it please your majesty,' replied the colonel, 'I know divers yeomanry men where for a night we may be welcome, and here is one who married my sister, whose house stands privately and out of the way'. 'Let us go thither,' saith the King.

"Whilst they were consulting this affair, Captain Thomas Gounter and Swan, my Lord Wilmot's man, rid scouting about Broadhalfpenny aforesaid, the colonel conducting the King, my Lord Wilmot and Colonel Robert Philips to his sister's house a private way and the backside of Hambledon, it being but half a mile from the place aforesaid.

"Alighting at the door, the colonel led them in, Lord Wilmot following, the King putting Colonel Robert Philips before him, saying, 'Thou lookest the most like a gentleman now.' Coming in, the colonel's sister met him; they all saluted her. She brought them into a little parlour where was a good fire. This was about candle-lighting.

"Wine, ale and biscuits were presently set before them, with a very cheerful countenance, as though the King's

1 Perhaps he felt that its security had been compromised: after all, Wilmot had made it his base for several days.

presence had some secret influence upon her, who suspected nothing less than that a king was present.[1] In an hour's space they went to supper, being all set promiscuously at a round table; and having half supped in comes the colonel's sister's husband, Mr. Thomas Symones, who, as it plainly appeared, had been in company that day. 'This is brave,' said he; 'A man can no sooner be out of the way but his house must be taken up with I know not whom.' And looking in the colonel's face, 'Is it you?' said he, 'You are welcome, and, as your friends, so they are all.'

"Passing round the table and viewing all the company, he said 'These are all Hydes now,'[2] but, peeping in the King's face, said of him 'Here is a Roundhead',[3] and, addressing his speech to the colonel, said, 'I never knew you to keep Roundheads' company before.' To which the colonel replied 'It is no matter; he is my friend, and I will assure you no dangerous man.' At which words he [Mr. Symons] clapt himself down in a chair next the King and took him by the hand, shaking him and saying, 'Brother Roundhead, for his sake thou art welcome' all the while believing the King to be so indeed, and making himself (whether for fear or in courtesy) to be one too, as well as he could act it, the King all the while complying with him, to all their admirations.

"Now and then he would swear before he was aware, for which the King reproved him, saying, 'Oh, dear brother, that is a 'scape; swear not, I beseech you.' Nevertheless, in that

[1] Colonel Gunter means that his sister had no idea of Charles's identity.

[2] In fact none of them were.

[3] Mr. Symons evidently based his conclusion on the King's appearance. The effects of William Penderel's barbering would certainly suggest an indifference to such mundane matters as personal neatness. And the Puritans in general professed a horror of long hair. His clothes would have supported this inference. According to Charles himself he was still wearing his Will Jackson suit; another early and generally reliable account ends a different description of his attire with the words: "somewhat like the meaner sort of country gentleman".

humour he was, he plied them hard with strong waters and beer."

This put the King in a difficulty. He didn't want to get drunk himself and he certainly didn't want to offend his host. He solved it by quickly passing his glass to his neighbour whenever Mr. Symons's head was turned the other way. Charles retained a vivid memory of his host who had "been all the day playing the good-fellow at an ale-house" and, after his Restoration, commemorated his hospitality with the appropriate gift of a punch bowl, ladle and set of drinking cups.

Meanwhile something had to be done to extricate the King from this unseasonable revelry. "It being ten of the clock the colonel began to bethink himself that the King had rid near forty miles that day, and was to undergo a very hard journey the next, and how to get the King out of his company and to his bed he could hardly devise; yet the colonel whispered his kinsman in the ear, saying, 'I wonder how thou shouldst judge so right; he is a Roundhead indeed, and if we could get him to bed the house were our own, and we could be merry.'

"He readily submitted, and the colonel presently, leaving Lord Wilmot behind, conducted the King and Colonel Robert Philips (who lay in the King's chamber) to bed."

How much longer the party went on is not recorded, but if Mr. Symons was disappointed in Charles's capacity for alcohol he was doubtless comforted by that of Lord Wilmot. At daybreak his unexpected guests made their farewells and set off towards Brighton – except for Colonel Phelips whom Charles, anxious as always to keep his escort down to those whose presence was strictly necessary, dismissed with thanks for his outstanding service. A few miles further on the same consideration led him to dispense with Thomas Gunter, so that the expedition finally consisted of the King, Wilmot, Robert Swan and Colonel Gunter.

The route they were following lay by Stansted, Houghton,

Arundel and Bramber. At Houghton they stopped at an inn
without getting off their horses for bread and beer, supple-
mented by a couple of ox tongues that the Colonel had
prudently appropriated from his sister's larder. At the top of
Arundel Hill the governor of the castle, Colonel Morley, an
officer who had played an important part in the Civil War in
Sussex and Hampshire, "met them full butt, hunting. The
colonel, the better to avoid them, it being a steep hill they
were going to go down, presently alighted and his company
(as was agreed before) did as he did, and so happily they
escaped them. The King, being told who it was, replied
merrily, 'I did not much like his starched mouchates'."
Coming into Bramber, a village where there was no reason to
expect military activity, they suddenly found the streets alive
with soldiers. Apparently a detachment had arrived the night
before with orders to guard Bramber bridge. "Luckily (or,
rather, by a special Providence)", Gunter records, "[They]
were just then come from their guard at Bramber Bridge into
the town for refreshment. We came upon them unawares and
were seen before we suspected anything.

"My Lord Wilmot was ready to turn back when I stepped
in and said 'If we do we are undone. Let us go on boldly and
we shall not be suspected.'

" 'He saith well' said the King. I went before, he followed,
and so passed through without any hindrance."

No incident could more neatly summarise the character of
those involved, or their relation to each other. Charles,
suddenly faced with danger, cool, collected and decisive;
Wilmot, probably suffering from a hangover, rattled and
futile; Gunter, for all his personal humility and instinctive
respect for his superiors in rank, not for a moment prepared
to put up with any nonsense from one who was the King's
intimate friend and his old commanding officer.

A few minutes after they had left Bramber a warning cough
from the King caused Gunter, who was riding on ahead, to

look round. A party of soldiers was pursuing them from Bramber at full gallop. It was a very ugly situation. They were riding through a narrow lane, so that even the desperate expedient of scattering was denied them. Gunter deliberately slackened his pace to allow the other two to come up with him. As they did so the soldiery crashed into them like a breaking wave "so that we could hardly keep our saddles for them, but passed by without any further hurt, being thirty or forty in number".

This second fright can hardly have done Wilmot's nerves any good. About half an hour later they reached Beeding, a village where Gunter had arranged for the King to refresh himself at a private house. "I was earnest that his Majesty should stay there awhile till I had viewed the coast; but my Lord Wilmot would by no means, for fear of those soldiers, but carried the King out of the road I knew not whither. So we parted. They where they thought safest, I to Brightemston, being agreed they should send to me when fixed anywhere and ready."

It was by this time between four and five in the afternoon. Brighton, then a small fishing village with only one inn, was only eight or nine miles away and the country empty and open. Wilmot's opportunities for making a hash of things would be limited, but it says a good deal for Colonel Gunter's strength of mind that he should be ready to ride on alone rather than allow himself to be overruled by a man whom he knew to be his inferior in tactical judgment and knowledge of the country. That he was too magnanimous to feel piqued or resentful is proved both by the warmth with which he writes of Wilmot and by the fact that he again ran great dangers to get him out of the country four years later.

That the others must have followed pretty close behind him is clear from his own narrative:

"Being come to the said Brightemston, I found all clear there, and the inn (the George[1]) free from all strangers at

[1] Not the same as the present hotel of that name.

that time. Having taken the best room in the house and bespoke
my supper, as I was entertaining myself with a glass of wine,
the King, not finding accommodation elsewhere to his mind,
was come to the inn; and up comes mine host (one Smith by
name), 'More guests,' saith he to me. He brought them up
into another room, I taking no notice. It was not long, but
drawing towards the King's room, I heard the King's voice,
saying aloud to my Lord Wilmot, 'Here, Mr. Barlow, I drink
to you.' 'I know that name,' said I to mine host, now by me.
'I pray inquire whether he was not a major in the King's army.'
Which done, he was found to be the man whom I expected,
and presently invited (as was likely) to the fellowship of a
glass of wine.''

From there it was an easy step for Gunter, who was
expecting the pleasure of Mr. Mansell's and Captain Tettersell's company at supper, to propose the merging of the two
parties in his own larger and more comfortable room. The
expected guests duly arrived and the stage was set for the
final scene.

XI

Success

As the light faded over a calm sea with a soft onshore breeze the company gathered at the George inn sat down to supper with every appearance of good fellowship. In this remote village on the way to nowhere they would be very unlucky if any inquisitive traveller were to turn up, and the chance of being disturbed by troop movements was unlikelier still. The master of the ship and the merchant who would know how to manage him had both kept their appointment punctually and there seemed no reason to expect a repetition of that agonising and still, to Charles and Wilmot, unexplained failure at Charmouth. None the less these unpleasant recollections and premonitions have a way of creeping in. Gunter noted with admiration: "At supper the King was cheerful, not shewing the least sign of fear or apprehension of any danger, neither then nor at any time during the whole course of this business, which is no small wonder." His most searching critics could not deny Charles the quality of composure. It was to be severely tried before the night was over.

The root of the trouble was that Tettersell, "the boatman" as Gunter calls him, had recognised the King. In 1648 a considerable part of the Channel fleet under Batten, irritated by the appointment of Colonel Rainborough to be its admiral, had revolted from the Parliament and sailed across to Holland. Charles, who was then in France, had joined it, together with Prince Rupert and other notables. Amongst other ineffective forays they captured a number of fishing vessels and coasters off Brighton and let them go again. One of these had been the *Surprise* with Tettersell in command. He might not take much interest in the larger issues of politics, but he would certainly not forget the face of the man who gave him back his ship. It was as well that his previous encounter with the King had left such happy memories, as his anger at finding himself (as he thought) tricked into so dangerous an enterprise would most likely have led him to walk out. As it was, he took Mansell aside after supper and roundly accused him of crooked dealing. It was the first that Mansell had heard of the real identity of the tall, dark, rather foreign-looking young man at the bottom of the table and he at last convinced Tettersell that he had acted towards him in good faith. But it was not an auspicious beginning.

While Mansell and Tettersell were conducting this conversation in an undertone, the rest of the company had begun to drift away from the table. Charles was standing with his back to the fire, leaning over a chair. He had observed at supper "that the master of the vessel looked very much upon me" and his recollection of similar symptoms in Pope, the Nortons' butler at Abbots Leigh, must have warned him that he had probably been recognised. But recognition came from an unexpected quarter. Smith, the innkeeper, who had been helping Robert Swan to wait at table and helping himself, one gathers, to the liquid refreshment, rushed up to Charles, seized his hand and kissed it, saying, "It shall not be said but I have kissed the best man's hand in England," adding, to make his meaning plainer: "God bless you wheresoever you go. I do not doubt, before I die, but to be a lord and my wife a lady." Charles accepted his homage with a laugh but, not wishing to confirm or deny its substance, walked off unconcernedly into the next room. He was quickly joined by a horrified Colonel Gunter, who earnestly begged his pardon and protested that as he himself had been guilty of no indiscretion so he could not imagine how the man knew. "Peace, peace, Colonel," cut in the King, "the fellow knows me and I him. He was one that belonged to the backstairs to my father. I hope he is an honest fellow."

Gunter, still somewhat upset, rejoined the others and began to question Tettersell about his arrangements. While they were talking the King came in and, opening the window, at once noticed that the wind had veered and was now blowing offshore. He pointed this out to Tettersell, and Gunter instantly offered to increase his payment by £10 if he would sail that night. Tettersell had already told Gunter that he had brought his ship into a creek for safety, where she was lying dry, and that they would have to wait for the morning tide to get her off. This offer of a bonus which even an idiot landsman must see he couldn't earn perhaps struck him as insulting. Perhaps it also prompted the thought that £60 was too modest a price for the passage of a man with £1000 on his head. At all events Tettersell became extremely truculent and demanded that in addition to the passage money Gunter should insure his ship for £200. This roused the Colonel's temper. "Argue it we did with him, how unreasonable it was, being so well paid etc., but to no purpose so that I yielded at last."

Flushed with triumph and no doubt with beer, which had been flowing very freely throughout the evening, the master went on to require the Colonel's bond. This was going too far. Gunter had shown earlier in the day that he would not give way to the King and Wilmot where he believed himself to be in the right. He was not going to be browbeaten by a beggarly boatman. "Moved with much indignation I began to be as resolute as he; saying among other things there were more boats to be had besides his; and if he would not act, another should, and made as though I would go to another."

Charles realised, if Tettersell did not, that Gunter was not bluffing. Unless he interposed on his side, and quickly, the Colonel was capable of calling the whole thing off. "He saith

[129]

right " (saith his majesty) , "A gentleman's word, especially before witnesses, is as good as his bond." Tettersell calmed down and was soon protesting eternal loyalty. "Carry them he would, what so ever came of it; and before he would be taken, he would run his boat under the water." It was settled that they should go on board that night and Tettersell went off to get his sea things and to knock up his crew, who were sleeping ashore in Brighton. He was then to return to the inn and they would all ride along the beach together to Shoreham.

While the master was gone Gunter persuaded Charles to lie down in his clothes and get some rest. Robert Swan saddled and bridled the horses and led them down quietly on to the shore. It was a clear night. Tettersell presently returned and the little party rode off.

When they reached the *Surprise*, which Charles, who was interested in ships, guessed (correctly) to be under sixty tons, Gunter took his leave, "craving his majesty's pardon if anything had happened through error, not want of will or loyalty; how willingly I would have waited further but for my family (being many) which would want me, and I hoped his majesty would not, not doubting but in a very little time he should be where he would". Gunter's only request was that the King should mention no names and give no details concerning his escape. "His majesty promised nobody should know." Not only did he keep his promise faithfully but he seems to have impressed even the garrulous Wilmot with the requirements of security.

Charles and Wilmot climbed up the ship's side on a ladder and immediately went below to the little cabin to lie doggo until they were at sea. "But I was no sooner got into the ship, and lain down upon the bed, but the master came in to me, fell down upon his knees, and kissed my hand; telling me that he knew me very well, and would venture life and all that he had in the world to set me down safe in France." Though

[130]

gratifying, this came as no surprise as Mansell had found opportunity to tell the King that Tettersell had in fact recognised him.

High water was at seven o'clock in the morning. About eight o'clock Gunter, who was still waiting nearby with the horses in case anything went wrong, saw them hoist sail. They were making good a course towards the Isle of Wight, as the ostensible pretext for Tettersell's voyage was to sell his coals at Poole. It was afternoon before they were out of sight. Gunter at last felt free to come off watch and return to his wife and family. Two hours after he had left Shoreham "Soldiers came thither in search for a tall, black man, six feet two inches high".

On board the *Surprise* everything was going swimmingly. Charles, as always, took a keen interest in the navigation and impressed the master with the degree of his professional knowledge. About five o'clock in the afternoon of Wednesday, October 15th, six weeks to the day since the Battle of Worcester, they altered course for France, leaving the Isle of Wight, still plainly visible, to starboard. Before the helm was put over one final piece of play-acting was required. Tettersell, intending to be ready with his story if any awkward questions were asked after he had got back to England, suggested that Charles should approach the crew and buy their support in persuading a seemingly reluctant captain to alter course for France. Charles made no difficulties about this. As the crew consisted of four men and a boy, the expense of the operation was negligible. And to explain his reasons for wanting to be put ashore in France he trotted out the story about two merchants, temporarily embarrassed but with money owing to them at Rouen, that Ellesdon and Colonel Wyndham had told to Limbry in the inn at Charmouth. The silver changed hands, Charles appealed to Tettersell, who growled something about his voyage being hindered, the crew lent their support to this decidedly odd-looking pair of businessmen, and the ship's head came round.

The wind blew due north all through the night, so all they had to do was run before it. Shortly before dawn they sighted the French coast. Almost at once the wind backed to south-west and the tide began to fail, so they anchored. With daylight they saw that they were within two miles of the shore, just off the little harbour of Fécamp. They were safe.

Or were they? Charles, with a true seaman's instinct, was keeping a sharp look-out. Just as the ebb-tide began to make he noticed a vessel to leeward "which, by her nimble working, I suspected to be an Ostend privateer". If she were, the situation was serious. France and Spain were then at war and Ostend, in the Spanish Netherlands, was the main base for attacking the trade of the French channel ports. Although in theory protected by a neutral flag, an English ship lying off a French port was fair game. If the Ostender caught them she would probably plunder the ship and either carry off everyone on board to some Spanish gaol or, worse still and more likely, land them at the nearest English port. Charles slipped down to the cabin to tell Wilmot of the danger and suggested that they should ask to be put ashore at once in the cock-boat. He had hardly got there before Tettersell appeared to tell him that he thought there was an Ostender in the offing. Charles, whose alertness and presence of mind one must salute for the last time, saw in a flash the danger that lay in confirming his opinion. Rather than risk his ship the captain might well haul up his anchor and, taking advantage of being to windward of the other vessel, sail for the coast of England while the going was good. He succeeded in convincing Tettersell that his fears were ground-less and, at the same time, persuaded him to send Wilmot and himself off in the cock-boat. It was a notable piece of diplomacy.

The cock-boat was manned by two of the seamen, one of whom, Richard Carver, completes the religious spectrum of those who helped the King in his hour of need. He was one of the earliest Quakers, and, as such, very far from any political or religious sympathy with Royalism. When they came to the beach Carver carried Charles ashore on his shoulders. Did Wilmot, for once, have to get his feet wet? History is silent on the point, but, given the circumstances, it seems a distinct possibility.

The minute the *Surprise* had got her boat back the wind began to blow with such violence from the south-east that Tettersell had to cut his cable. (He subsequently presented Colonel Gunter with a bill for £8 to replace his anchor, which was duly paid.) If the master could have commanded a wind to carry him direct to Poole, he would have chosen no other. It held till he arrived off the port, and such was the speed he made across the Channel that no one had any reason to suspect that his course from Shoreham had been so circuitous. Exceptional luck with the wind on both outward and homeward passages had enabled Tettersell to cover his traces completely.

The King and Wilmot spent the first day of their liberty at Fécamp trying to hire horses to take them to Rouen. Their general appearance and their having no luggage or even a clean shirt between them can hardly have helped. Apart from the fact that Charles discovered that the supposed Ostend privateer was simply a harmless French hoy, nothing is recorded of the twenty-four hours they passed there. Next morning they successfully obtained horses and rode to Rouen, where they intended to put up at an inn in the fish-market, one of the best in the town. The management, understandably, did not like the look of them and refused them accommodation until an English merchant, whom Charles sent for, came and vouched for them. Even then some doubts must have lingered, since Charles on his next and very different Channel crossing in May 1660 told Pepys that "at Rouen . . . the people went into the rooms before he went away to see whether he had not stole something or other''. The King's old tutor and chaplain, Dr. Earle, hearing of his master's arrival, hurried round to the hotel. Meeting Charles he asked him if he could take him to the King. That a man who had known him intimately since boyhood and had shared his exile should not recognise him when he was looking for him is the most eloquent evidence possible of his worn and tattered appearance.

From Rouen Charles sent the first news of his safety to his mother at the French court. He and Wilmot bought some new clothes and hired a coach in which they set out for Paris early on October 19th. They stopped one night on the road and entered Paris late in the evening of the 20th. They had been met a few miles from the city by Queen Henrietta Maria, James, Duke of York, the Duc d'Orléans and other nobles who escorted them in triumph to the Louvre. Thus the news of his escape was officially released to the world.

It seems to have come as a complete surprise to the Government and Press of England. On October 13th the Council of State had informed Captain John Ley that "there are strong probabilities that Charles Stuart and the Duke of Buckingham[1] were in or about Staffordshire some days after the victory at Worcester, and probably they may still be in those parts under disguise''. They enclosed a warrant empowering him to search for them and bring them before the Governor of Stafford or any other Justice of the Peace. On October 14th they directed the Committee of Examinations to question a certain prisoner in London about Charles Stuart. They also sent out a general warning to Customs Officers that Charles Stuart and the Duke of Buckingham were still in England "obscured and under disguise, expecting a fit time to pass into foreign parts''. On the same day they enclosed the results of an interrogation,

---

[1] Buckingham had been among the party who rode with the King from Worcester to Whiteladies. He succeeded in making his escape to the Continent independently.

perhaps the one they had ordered that morning, to the Governor of Stafford, ordering him "to send for and examine the persons therein mentioned as to concealing and carrying away Charles Stuart and the Duke of Buckingham".

The Press had risen above the Government's plodding and unimaginative preoccupation with the immediate vicinity of the Battle of Worcester, but its speculations, though closer to the spirit of events, were as uninformed by accurate intelligence. On October 22nd the *Scout* printed, somewhat sceptically, a report of the King's arrival in Holland. It preferred the belief that he was shipped from the Thames on October 14th to France or Flanders. On the 28th the *Weekly Intelligencer* under the summary of news for the 23rd retracted the information published in its previous number that Charles had landed in Holland. It was now confirmed from the Hague that his sister knew nothing of him. On the 29th *A Perfect Account* reported hopefully amongst the items for the 28th that a ship bound for Holland that had recently been lost with all hands might have had Charles on board. "Time", it added prudently, "may discover the truth thereof." About the same time a pamphlet giving the text of the Earl of Derby's speech from the scaffold before his execution on the preceding Wednesday, October 15th, carried the alluring headline, not made good in the contents, "likewise the manner how the King of Scots took shipping at Graves-end on the fourth of this instant October, with Captain Hind, disguised in sea-mens Apparel and safely arrived at the Hague in Holland".

On October 30th the news broke. The weekly *Several Proceedings in Parliament* carried a letter from Paris dated October 21st reporting Charles's arrival. He was further said to have told Henrietta Maria and others of his escape by way of London and Flushing. On the same day *Mercurius Politicus*, the weekly newspaper edited by Marchamont Nedham, the most entertaining journalist of his time, printed a despatch from Paris dated October 22nd giving a clear and detailed account of Charles's arrival and adding that he had told the Duke of Orleans "that he went up and down London in a gentlewoman's habit". The issue, since it covered the week October 23rd–30th, also contained a despatch from Leyden, dated October 16th, which asserted that Charles had arrived in Holland and was lying low. As an example of Nedham's agreeably irreverent approach, employed irrespectively of whether he happened, at that moment, to be serving the Royalist or the Parliamentary cause, it deserves quotation:

"It appears that the young Duck is as good at diving as the old. I do not like it, for it seems to me they march to one end who thus take one away. Tarquin (as you call him) who being hunted, ducked at Worcester is risen at Scheveling where being come two Things made him pop down his head and play Bopeep again: The one having no clothes, no George, nor Periwig . . . he is ashamed. The other is this, our States have enacted that no King or forreigne Prince shall come upon their ground without first giving notice and warning to them . . .

"The Courtiers say the King and Buckingham were conducted by a Thiefe to London in disguise, whence after two hours stay they got to a Pink[1] and so made to our coast . . .

"Now the Royal Party give out; the King will betake himself to Denmark and Sweden for succours, to try another fall in Scotland . . . both these Crownes have other ways to imploy their money and men."

The version of Charles's adventures that was to claim general acceptance received its definitive shape in a despatch from Paris dated October 23rd. Printed in most of the newspapers in identical terms, it also formed the substance of a number of broadsides which appear early in November, such as that published by Robert Ibbitson, *A Mad Designe or a description of the King of Scots marching in his Disguise after the rout at Worcester, with the particulars where He was and what He and his company did every day and night after He fled from*

[1] A small, flat-bottomed sailing ship.

Worcester. Only the most perfunctory efforts were made to fulfil this shamelessly bogus prospectus. Such details of human interest as appear are of a kind that the feeblest imagination could easily supply. On September 4th, for instance, the day after the Battle of Worcester, Charles, accompanied by Wilmot and the Duke of Buckingham, approached a house in Cheshire that stood alone to ask for victuals. "Some pow-thered Beefe was brought to them and the Scots King drunke off a Flaggon of Beere, and with a peece of bread in one hand and of beefe in the other . . . marched into the borders of Lancashire and all that day after lay close in a hollow tree . . . On the 4th September at night they . . . went a Pilgrimage all that night on foot.

"The next day September 5th they betook themselves to hide them in a Wood . . . and got some Hips and Hawes.

"On September 6th they came to a Shepherds Tent who told them of a Lady in which they had some confidence living near."

And so on. Stripped of its feeble efforts at authentic detail the story runs briefly as follows. Wilmot went to see the lady, who took them disguised as mounted servants to Bristol. "The Scots King rid before the Lady on one horse, the Duke of Buckingham before her Gentlewoman upon another horse, and the Lord Wilmot as her Groome upon an Horse by himselfe." They got to Bristol about the middle of September, but hearing so much talk in the inn where they were staying of the search that was being made for them they headed for London, where they arrived about September 20th. During their stay Charles, escorted by the lady, went on several depressing and pointless sight-seeing expeditions. He saw the prisoners from his beaten army encamped in Tothill Fields; he went to Westminster Hall and saw the captured Scottish Colours taken from his father and himself. At last Wilmot found a vessel of some forty tons in the Thames whose Captain agreed to smuggle three gentlemen over to France for £120. They embarked at Gravesend about the middle of October, whereupon the

Captain promptly recognised the King and demanded more money. As soon as this was paid they set sail and landed without further incident at Le Havre.

The only points at which this narrative approaches the truth are, with the single exception of the ship's Captain recognising his passenger, towards the beginning. Charles did indeed make a pilgrimage on foot on the night of September 4th; he did hide in woods and he did spend a day in a tree, though not inside its hollow trunk. Does this suggest some breach of security? Probably not. Given the nature of the countryside into which he was known to have fled, anyone could have guessed as much. On the other hand, the description of the journey to Bristol is much too close to the Jane Lane episode to be so easily dismissed. Someone must have talked. And if it was not the King it must have been Wilmot. That Charles was extremely careful to give fabricated accounts of his adventures we have abundant evidence. It seems probable that he studied the earlier reports of his exploits in the English Press and built his own fictions on those foundations. Certainly he told his mother that he had been much assisted by a highwayman and flattered the popular misconception that he had spent a great deal of his time in London dressed as a woman. To some versions he added a number of geographical flourishes: the Venetian ambassador in Paris reported that "he reached the extremity of Scotland" (travelling on foot and by night) before the absence of shipping forced him to make his way to London. And Mademoiselle de Montpensier, who questioned him closely about his experiences, records in her memoirs the far from truthful account he gave her. In supplying misleading reports of his travels and in winning general acceptance for them Charles kept faith with Gunter and the others who had trusted his silence. He kept their secrets until on his Restoration he was in a position to reward their service. If he had on several occasions saved himself by the readiness of his tongue, he saved his friends by knowing how to restrain it.

[138]

XII

Rewards for Service

INGRATITUDE IS a charge that is often levelled against the
Stuarts in general and Charles II in particular. It did not,
however, disfigure the King's conduct towards the men
and women who had helped him to escape when, nine years
later, he came into his own again. As soon as the tide began to
run in his favour he was inundated with petitions and requests
from those who claimed to have served the Royalist cause.
There is a pleasant story that, a month or two before he returned
to England, he received a deputation of such persons and,
after listening gravely to their recital, called for a bottle of
wine. He filled a glass, drank their healths, and said that he
was now even with them as he had done as much for them as
they had ever done for him. No doubt he was pressed by a
number of false and impudent claims. No doubt the general
agreement to let bygones be bygones on which the Restoration
settlement was founded meant that he could not recompense
all those whose loyalty to the Crown had cost them dear,
even if he wished to do so. No doubt his lavishness towards his
avaricious and odious mistresses presents an unattractive
contrast to his treatment of men whose fidelity was not for
sale. All this is of a piece with the man Charles had become.
But the story of the escape from Worcester, still more its
importance to the King, has to do with the man he might once
have liked to be. And the people involved were treated
accordingly.

The first scene of that story, the city of Worcester, yields but one claimant, whose hopefulness compels a certain admiration. When the Cromwellians broke into the town they arrested a young medical student named Thomas Cock in mistake for the King. Nine years later Cock had apparently not succeeded in satisfying the medical examiners and petitioned for a royal writ to the University of Oxford to grant him the Degree of Doctor of Medicine as a compensation for his sufferings in the royal cause.

Of those who conducted the King from Worcester to Whiteladies, Francis Yates, who had acted as guide, had been executed at Oxford shortly afterwards for refusing to say what he knew about the King's movements. His widow was granted an annuity of £50, as was his elder son, and his younger son received £20 a year. His master, Charles Giffard, the landlord of the Boscobel estate, received a pension of £300.

The Penderels, as was fitting, were treated with exceptional liberality. Their pensions were to be paid in perpetuity, that is, with remainder to their heirs for ever. To safeguard this arrangement from the meddling of parsimonious governments or the folly of spendthrift Penderels a trust was set up from which the money is still paid. The ramifications of descent from five brothers and one sister over a period of more than three centuries have led, as might have been expected, to a far-flung distribution of the royal bounty. By the end of the nineteenth century several citizens of the United States were in receipt of these pensions and one of the French ambassadors to the court of Queen Victoria had the necessary genealogical qualifications. Over and above the pensions the family also received sums of money and personal gifts from the King, who welcomed them to court soon after his Restoration and commanded that they should pay him an annual visit. Help was given in apprenticing their children and setting them up in their chosen trades. Humphrey's grandson was a godson of the Queen, Catherine of Braganza, and was sent to Rome to be educated at the Jesuit College. On graduating he was released from his vows in order that he could become a secret agent of the Stuarts, then once more in exile, and ended his days as a Sardinian Marquis with the title of Penderel di Boscobello. The Penderels enjoyed, like their co-religionists, Carlis, Huddleston, Whitgreave and Giffard, the privilege of exemption from the Test Act and other measures against the recusants. This immunity was extended to their descendants by George I and George II, so that the Marquis Penderel di Boscobello was, when in England, enabled to pursue his profession without undue interference. Of the old, original generation one, William, is said to have survived into the reign of William III.

Mr. Woolf of Madeley declined a pension, as he was in easy circumstances, but accepted an augmentation to his grant of arms which would commemorate the loyalty of his family. Colonel Carlis, who had found it necessary to flee the country because of the conspicuous part he had played in the Battle of Worcester, had joined the King in exile and returned with him in 1660. In addition to a grant of arms, of which the oak was a prominent feature, the family name was changed to Carlos.[1] Besides these honours he received a one-third share of the proceeds of a tax on all straw and hay brought into the cities of London and Westminster and, no doubt to facilitate its collection, the office of Inspector of Livery Horsekeepers. He was also given an occasional *douceur* from the Secret Service money.

Mr. Whitgreave of Moseley Hall was characteristically diffident in claiming a reward. Not until six years after the Restoration did he petition the King, who at once granted him an annuity of £200 with remainder to his son. It is strange that he should have made so little impression on Charles. When he was dictating his account to Pepys in 1680 the King confused his name with that of a meadow outside Worcester on which he had reviewed his troops and called him Mr. Pitchcroft.

[1] See p. 37.

Both he and Father Huddleston had thought it prudent to go away from Moseley for some weeks after the King's departure, but, finding that no search was made for them, they returned home and lived unmolested.

At some date before the Restoration Father Huddleston had become a member of the Benedictine order. In 1660 Charles provided him with quarters in Somerset House where he could enjoy, under the protection of Queen Henrietta Maria, immunity from religious persecution. After her death in 1669 he was made one of the chaplains to Queen Catherine, which not only preserved his privileges but carried a small salary to which a pension was added. In 1671 he and another Benedictine monk paid a visit to the University of Oxford where they were well received, meeting, amongst others, Anthony à Wood, the historian and antiquary, who heard Huddleston's story "with very great delight" and urged him to set it down in writing for posterity's sake. But his chief reward was to come on Charles II's deathbed. As the King lay dying his brother James bent down and in a whisper asked him if he did not desire to be reconciled to the Church of Rome. The King's answer "With all my heart" was heard by others in the room who had not heard the question. At once James had the room cleared and the doors locked. The next step was to find an English-speaking priest; of those about the court the Queen's were Portuguese and the Duchess of York's Italian. James, on the advice of Barillon, the French ambassador, had just decided to send to the Venetian Resident's house when another diplomat, the Count of Castelmelhor, happened to notice Huddleston among the Queen's compatriots. He was smuggled up the backstairs and welcomed by the King as one who had once saved his life and was now come to save his soul. He heard his confession and administered the last sacraments. Did the dying man remember the little chapel at Moseley Hall with its cross and candlesticks and recall his eager acceptance of the arguments put forward in the book written by Huddleston's uncle? It was more than thirty years ago, more than half his lifetime, and he had only a few hours left to live.

Huddleston outlived all his companions in the adventures of 1651, dying in 1698 at the age of ninety. His neighbours at Bentley Hall, Colonel Lane and his famous sister Jane, had received the most generous recognition of all those involved in the escape. Alarmed at the uncomfortably accurate account of the King's journey to Bristol,[1] they had themselves escaped to France and were welcomed to Paris by Charles himself in December 1651. Jane Lane remained abroad until the Restoration, but her brother had returned to England by 1654 and was imprisoned together with his old father, though it is not clear whether they suffered for their part in the King's escape or for some other Royalist activity. In 1660 Jane Lane was voted £1,000 by Parliament to buy a jewel and was granted a pension of £1,000 a year by the King. Several letters from Charles show that he always held her in special affection and respect. She married late in life Sir Clement Fisher of Packington, the host of Wilmot and her brother on the hawking expedition that had given them a pretext for keeping an eye on the royal party as it set out from Bentley. Colonel Lane himself was offered a peerage, but declined. He accepted a pension of £500 a year, which was extended after his death to his son. All his daughters received a marriage portion of £1,000 apiece and the Colonel himself received a further gift of £2,000 in the year of his death. A monument to him in St. Peter's, Wolverhampton, was erected at the expense of the Government.

If the treatment of the Lanes was princely, that of the Nortons appears to have been somewhat cool. There is no record of their being offered any reward for their hospitality, though of course it is possible that such an offer was made and declined. They were, it is true, in a different category from

[1] See p. 138.

the Lanes or the Wyndhams in that they were unaware of the identity of their guest and consequently precluded from making any special efforts on his behalf. This, however, was certainly not true of their butler, Pope. Since his name does not appear among those who enjoyed the King's bounty it seems almost certain that he must have died before the Restoration.

The Wyndhams of Trent were well rewarded for their outstanding services. Colonel Wyndham, like Jane Lane, was voted £1,000 to buy a jewel and was shortly afterwards created a baronet and given a pension of £600. Generous as this was, there was more to come: in 1670 he was paid the huge sum of £10,800. His wife also received a pension of £400 and the two maids who had waited on the King pensions of £50 together with an outright gift of £100 apiece. Henry Peters, Wyndham's servant, who had proved such an invaluable guide and courier, was made Yeoman of the Field, that is, one of the King's personal servants, and Robert Swan, Wilmot's old manservant, who had shared the King's adventures from Trent to Shoreham, was given a pension of £80 a year. Julian Coningsby, now married to a Mr. Hext, received a pension of £200.

As we have seen, there was some doubt as to who, if anyone, should be distinguished by any mark of royal favour for the fiasco at Charmouth. Stephen Limbry seems to have had sense enough not to invite a snub by tendering a bill for the services he had been unavoidably prevented from rendering. But Captain Ellesdon, whose visit to Sir Hugh Wyndham's house at Pilsdon when the hunt was up for the King laid his conduct open to a most sinister interpretation, had no such inhibitions. His solicitation for a pension payable out of the Customs of the port of Lyme was coldly received: but, after some years, supported by the testimony of Colonel Wyndham that "he honestly endeavoured to procure a vessel for his majesty's transportation after the battle of Worcester; that the shipmaster with whom he contracted failed, but he was

[144]

not in the least degree guilty and should have some bounty", he was granted a pension of £100 with reversion to his two sons. If Charles and Clarendon were prepared to give him the benefit of the doubt, no such indulgence was acceptable to his old enemy Captain Alford. The animosity between the two families was no doubt rooted in a local struggle for power to which the wider issues of the Civil War were merely incidental. Thirty years after the Charmouth episode they were still at it. A last glimpse of them in 1681 shows Alford doing his best to get Ellesdon into trouble for his alleged tenderness towards dissenters.

Of those who were instrumental in the ultimate success of the escape, Dr. Henchman was rewarded by preferment in the Church to which his character and learning were in any case a sufficient title.[1] Mrs. Hyde of Heale must have died before the Restoration, as it is inconceivable that the King would have neglected to honour a kinswoman of his Chancellor who had entertained him at such a risk to herself. Colonel Robert Phelips, who had continued his conspiratorial activities in the Royalist cause, was arrested by the Commonwealth Government in the autumn of 1653 and imprisoned in the Tower. Escaping in December of that year, he joined the King in exile. At the Restoration he was made Groom of the Bedchamber and sat as M.P. for Stockbridge from 1660–1 and for Andover in 1685. James II made him Chancellor of the Duchy of Lancaster in 1687, but with the changes of the Glorious Revolution he lost the office. He long outlived his friends and comrades of 1651, dying in 1707 at the great age of eighty-nine.

His greatest friend, Colonel George Gunter, did not live to see the Restoration. The place and date of his death are unknown, but almost certainly it took place abroad about the year 1659. The fact that there is no memorial of him or record of his burial at Racton, where the family continued to live till the middle of the eighteenth century, is strong evidence for

[1] See below, p. 102.

his having died in exile. And in the narrative that he composed as his own death was approaching his sorrowful reference to Wilmot's death, which occurred early in 1658, as having taken place some little time before, is good evidence for the date. If his parting from his wife and young children was necessitated by the help he had given that nobleman in his second escape from England in 1655, it is typical of his magnanimity that he should speak of him only with affection. His widow, left with an estate that had been squeezed dry in the Royalist cause, petitioned the King on behalf of herself and her children. Charles granted her a pension of £200 a year and immediately had her second son, George, sent to Winchester. In 1664 he intimated to the Warden and Fellows of New College that he would like the boy elected to the first scholarship that should fall vacant, a request with which that body wisely complied. The eldest son, Thomas, was sent to Magdalen Hall and the youngest, John, who had been a baby in the autumn of 1651 when his mother sat up night after night listening for the sound of hooves and the stable door opening, was admitted a member of Corpus Christi College in 1668. In the distressed state of the family fortunes it seems impossible that the three boys could have been sent to their father's old university without assistance, and it is reasonable to suppose that the governing bodies of Magdalen Hall and Corpus received a hint from the King. Indeed it is probable that he helped the family in more ways than we know of, since George Gunter was elected M.P. for Chichester in James II's Parliament, a fact that suggests that their financial situation was by no means desperate, the adjective employed by his mother in her original petition to the King. His gratitude to the family extended also to the son of Captain Thomas Gunter, who was appointed by royal recommendation to the Recordership of Devizes.

Colonel Gunter's acquaintance Francis Mansell, the Chichester merchant, was rewarded with a post in the Customs at

Southampton worth £60 a year. In 1661 he petitioned the King that the expenses he incurred in having to take flight after the escape had been great and that the receipts of his small office were insufficient compensation. Charles granted him a pension of £200 a year, but when Pepys met him in an inn in London in 1667 he was in abject poverty, having received no payment for four years past. Mansell's experience was a common one. A list of arrears drawn up in 1685 shows that on average the payments were over two years behind. Mansell himself was then just under two years in arrears, but Captain Ellesdon had received nothing for nearly seven years.

Captain Nicholas Tettersell did extremely well out of his voyage to Fécamp. Soon after the Restoration he brought the *Surprise* up the Thames and moored her off Whitehall, partly as a public attraction, partly to remind the King of his services. Charles took the hint. In July 1660 she was refitted at Deptford dockyard, entered in the Royal Navy as a fifth-rate, renamed the *Royal Escape* and provided with an establishment of wages for a commander and two seamen. Tettersell himself was given the command of another fifth-rate, the *Sorlings*, and in 1661 was appointed Captain of the frigate *Monk*, a third-rate. Besides this he was granted in 1663 a pension of £100 a year with remainder to his immediate family for ninety-nine years. His fortunes suffered a temporary check when in June 1667 he was guilty of some unspecified misconduct, but in 1671 he was appointed to the command of his old ship the *Royal Escape*. As she carried no guns and served simply as a naval yacht or despatch vessel, he was not required to discharge the duties of the post, which, with its emoluments was further made heritable by his son. He settled down at Brighton, where he died in 1674. The inscription on his tombstone attributing the King's escape solely to his prudence, valour and loyalty might have struck Colonel Gunter as somewhat excessive.

The mate of the *Surprise*, Richard Carver, the Quaker who

carried the King ashore at Fécamp on his shoulders, obtained the noblest reward of all. He made no approach to the King until 1669 because, as he himself said, "he did what he did to relieve a man in distress" and consequently desired no reward. He was however impelled to action by his sympathy for the members of his Society who were imprisoned for their beliefs. On obtaining an audience he asked the King for liberty for Friends and produced a list of a hundred and ten who had been in prison for six years. "So the King took the paper . . . and said there were many of them, and that they would be in again in a month's time; and that the country gentlemen complained to him that they were so troubled with Quakers. So he said he would release him six: but the Friend thinks to go to him again for he had not fully relieved himself."

This account of the interview between Charles and Richard Carver comes from a letter written to Margaret Fox, the wife of George Fox, the Society's founder. Carver pursued his intention and saw the King again in February 1670, when he obtained the promise of a pardon for four hundred and seventy-one Friends and twenty other Nonconformists, among them John Bunyan. Was the release of the author of *Pilgrim's Progress* an indirect consequence of the royal escape or was it a by-product of the policy of religious toleration towards which Charles always leaned?[1] Or would it be having it both ways to say that the kindness he had met with from those who had suffered religious persecution when he was a hunted man in the autumn of 1651 had nourished one of the few consistent and admirable principles that can be extracted from his life and conduct?

[1] Bunyan was released in the spring of 1672 at the time of the Declaration of Indulgence.

Note on Sources

ALTHOUGH A number of the people involved in the escape, including the King himself, wrote or dictated accounts of these events, they did not, for obvious reasons, do so at the time. Except for the letter of the unknown Royalist prisoner at Chester, the minutes and orders of the Council of State and the (mostly inaccurate) reports in the newspapers, all the authorities I have used date therefore from after 1660 and some from a good way after. Charles, for instance, did not dictate his account to Pepys until 1680, and internal evidence suggests that Whitgreave set down his narrative at about the same time. Furthermore, some important witnesses, such as the Penderels, were illiterate so that their evidence is to be found in what are, strictly speaking, secondary sources such as the tracts and broadsides that appeared soon after the Restoration. It is easy to see, by comparing these secondary sources with the first-hand accounts, that some of their authors had obtained information about places, names and dates which could only have come from careful and critical inquiry in the relevant quarter. Thus the evidence of the Penderel family can, with reasonable certainty, be deduced from the first three printed sources listed below.

A complete bibliography of the subject is available (W. A. Horrox, *Bibliography of Literature relating to the escape and preservation of Charles II after the battle of Worcester*, Aberdeen, 1924). As this work lists all the references in the Calendar of State Papers Domestic, the only source for the measures taken by the Government to catch the King and the main source for the information about pensions and rewards, I shall not give them. The present list and its annotations is intended simply to serve the purpose defined in the Preface. All the principal sources are printed in one or more of the following works:

(1) Hughes, J. (ed.), *The Boscobel Tracts* (Edinburgh and London, 2nd ed. 1857).

(2) Fea, Allan, *The Flight of the King* (London, 1897).

(3) Fea, Allan, *After Worcester Fight* (London, 1904).

(4) Broadley, A. M., *The Royal Miracle* (London, 1912).

The numbers preceding these titles will be used as references, so that the reader can easily find where any given source is available in print.

I. MANUSCRIPT

1. Pepysian Library MSS 2141.[1] The King's Narrative (1), (3).

In addition to the original shorthand taken by Pepys at the King's dictation and a long-hand transcription prepared under Pepys's supervision, this MS contains the following sources:

> Colonel Robert Phelips' Notes
> Father Huddleston's Notes
> Father Huddleston's *Brief Account*

This agrees substantially with the account he wrote in collaboration with Whitgreave (see below).

> Captain Alford's Narrative (2) and (4).

Discussed in text.

> Letter from unknown Royalist prisoner at Chester (1).

As in the B.M. transcript, this letter bears the headnote "A Relation of the King's Escape as taken from the Queen Mother

---

[1] I wish to express my thanks to the Master and Fellows of Magdalene College, Cambridge, for permitting me to consult this MS. A full transcript of all the material supplementary to the King's narrative is to be found in B.M. Add. MSS 31955.

1651 by Sir Richard Brown then Resident at Paris and prepared for the Press''. It is thus open to objection as a Royalist hand-out.

2. Bodleian Library English Historical MSS c.51 contains Colonel Robert Phelips's Account (4).

This differs in treatment but not in substance from his Notes in Pepysian Library MSS 2141. Though undated it cannot have been written earlier than 1663, as it refers to Henchman's tenure of the see of London.

3. B.M. Add. MSS 9008. Colonel Gunter's Narrative (2).

The manuscript must date from 1660–3 as it mentions ''Dr. Hinchman, now the right Reverend Bishop of Salisbury''. It begins in the third person but later switches to the first and bears the superscription ''By Colonell Gounter . . . as it was taken from his mouth by a person of worth, a little before his death''.

4. East Sussex County Record Office, Lewes. Shiffner MS 3562.

This small MS volume is of no value. As the Shiffner MSS have only recently been calendared I list it simply to save others the trouble of reading it. It is an eighteenth-century compilation copied from two printed sources (Nos. 6 and 12 below), occasionally enlivened by explosions of High Tory wrath against Dissenters and Latitudinarians.

II. Printed Sources

A. *Contemporary*

1. *White-Ladies* (London, 1660) (4).

2. *A True Narrative and relation of His Majesty's Miraculous Escape from Worcester* (London, 1660) (2).

Both end with the King's arrival at Moseley. Their claims

to be based on first-hand accounts are supported by their high degree of local knowledge.

3. *Boscobel* by Thomas Blount (London, 1660, 1662) (1) and (3).

Divided into two parts of which the first part, concluding with the King's arrival at Bentley, was published in 1660. The complete work, taking the story to his arrival in Paris, was published in 1662. There are several later editions.

Blount's *Boscobel* is much the best single account of the whole affair. A Catholic lawyer whose family came from Worcestershire, he was well equipped to discover the early stages of the story: in addition to personal inquiries he may have made use of the first two sources listed above.

A certain mystery surrounds the work. At first it was given almost the status of what would now be called an official history by a written expression of the King's approval and, indeed, exclusive licence. But in 1662 the King publicly declared that it "hath divers errors and mistakes in it, and [is] therefore not to be admitted as a true and perfect narrative". The mystery is deepened by the fact that Blount himself twice denied the authorship of the book.[1] This does not, of course, vitiate the scrupulous care and accuracy of the book, which can easily be tested by comparing it with sources not available to its writer.

4. *Miraculum Basilicon* by A[braham] J[enings] (London, 1664) (4).

A racy and entertaining account which discloses some special knowledge, particularly of the Charmouth incident.

5. Whitgreave's narrative (1) and (3).

[1] For a full exposition of the question and citation of authorities see Fea, *After Worcester Fight*, pp. xiv–xv.

6. Whitgreave and Huddleston, *A Summary of Occurrences relating to the Miraculous Preservation of Our Late Sovereign Lord, King Charles II, after the Defeat of his Army at Worcester in the year* 1651 (London, 1688) (2).

7. Huddleston, *Brief Account* (London, 1688).

All three confine themselves to the Moseley episode.

8. Anne Wyndham, *Claustrum Regale Reseratum or the King's Concealment at Trent* (London, 1667) (1) and (3).

W. A. Horrox (*op. cit.*) records that in Anne Wyndham's own copy there is a MS note that the book was written for her by Colonel Bullen Reynes [Reymes] of Whaddon, her brother-in-law, whom Wilmot resembled so closely.

9. Captain Ellesdon's letter to Lord Clarendon (1), (3) and (4).

10. Captain Alford's narrative (2) and (4).

Both these sources for the Charmouth incident are discussed in the text.

11. The contemporary newspapers which I have quoted are to be found in the Thomason tracts in the British Museum (E.641 (14) (24) (25) (27), E.643 (19), E.644, E.645 (5), E.787, E.788, 669 f.16).

12. Bate, George, M.D., *Elenchi motuum nuperorum in Anglia* (London, 1661–3). Originally published in Latin, but relevant extracts from the English edition printed in (2).

Bate was Charles II's doctor, and in his account which covers the whole affair he claims to have set down the story as he had heard it from the King after his restoration. It is thus earlier than the account dictated to Pepys (listed above as the King's narrative), but its author had not a tenth of Pepys's curiosity or critical intelligence, and his standards of accuracy are not high.

13. Clarendon, *History of the Rebellion*, extracts printed in (1).

Although Clarendon no doubt heard at first-hand the full story of the King's adventures within a few weeks of their taking place, he did not in fact write this part of his great work until he was himself again an exile in France nearly twenty years later. He was thus without the means of verifying his facts or refreshing his astonishing memory, so that his account, through no fault of his own, is muddled and unreliable. His judgements of the people involved are as always of the greatest interest and value.

B. *Modern Works*

Apart from those already mentioned in the Preface, both C. J. Lyon, *Personal History of Charles II 1650–1* (Edinburgh, 1851), and Eva Scott, *The King in Exile* (London, 1905), are sound and scholarly. Raymond Craufurd, *The Last Days of Charles II* (Oxford, 1909) and the authorities there cited, is my principal source for the final scene with Father Huddleston.

Index

Index

(See Detail)

R. Severn

MADELEY

Bentley H.

STOURBRIDGE

KIDDERMINSTER

WORCESTER

0   10   20   30   40
Miles

CIRENCESTER

ABBOTS LEIGH   BRISTOL

Stonehenge

CASTLE CARY   MERE

TRENT

BROADWINDSOR

CHARMOUTH   BRIDPORT